CINNAMON BUNS AND MILK BONE UNDERWEAR

AND OTHER WHIMSICAL WANDERINGS

JAMES SCOTT BELL

Copyright © 2026 by James Scott Bell

All rights reserved.

No part of this book may be reproduced in any form or by any electronic or mechanical means, including information storage and retrieval systems, without written permission from the author, except for the use of brief quotations in a book review.

Compendium Press
Woodland Hills, CA

ISBN: 978-0-910355-67-4

PRAISE FOR JAMES SCOTT BELL

Some of us have to ponder before we pontificate, but James Scott Bell can produce a paragraph of clever quips faster than Oscar Wilde or Dorothy Parker. In Cinnamon Buns and Milk Bone Underwear you'll find some of his best whimsical wanderings. Guaranteed to make you smile!

ANGELA HUNT, NEW YORK TIMES BESTSELLING WRITER

Every time one of James Scott Bell's Whimsical Wanderings arrives in my email box, I smile, even before I open it. Each post takes me down a path I am not expecting but am so glad for the journey by the time I reach the end. If you want to lift your spirits while being surprised by how one thought can lead to another, treat yourself to this book!

ROBIN LEE HATCHER, CHRISTY AWARD WINNING AUTHOR OF *THE BRITISH ARE COMING* SERIES

Only James Scott Bell can take an ordinary (or off-the-wall) reference and turn it into a fascinating (or laugh-out-loud) tale. Immensely readable and unputdownable.

DEBORAH RANEY, AUTHOR OF *A NEST OF SPARROWS* AND *WHO TOUCHES THE MOUNTAINS*

CONTENTS

Running With the White Rabbit	vii
Do Not Go Hatless Into That Good Night	1
For a Healthy Marriage, Don't Be This	4
Harpoons and Hemorrhoids	7
Harmonicas and Husbands	11
Einstein's Box Top and DiMaggio's Disappearance	15
Cinnamon Buns, Wilt the Stilt, and Bill Walton's Beard	19
Of Baseball, Bronx, and Bluster	23
Troupers, Lovers, and Aunt Bebe's Bean Bowl	28
Chewing Gum, The Gumm Sisters, and Gumming Up the Works	32
This Chapter is Not Made of Genuine Fiberglas	36
Honor, Duty, and Monkeyshines	40
Signs—I Mean Billboards—of the Times	44
Spiders, Myths, and Burt Lancaster's Teeth	50
Take Me Out to the Old Ballgame With The Andrews Sisters	56
Fertilizer Discipline	60
The Day I Met the All-American Girl	63
Driving a Fire Hazard to The Prom	68
Growing Wings on the Way Down	71
Chest Hair, Hot Dogs, and Wienie Whistles	76
At Least I Was Ready for My New York Moment	81
Punny You Should Ask	86
Will the Truth Set You Free?	91
Boxing, Grilling, and Octopi	96

What Tom Selleck and I Have in Common	101
Kisses, Marriage, and the Death of Johnny Stompanato	106
Marketing Lessons My Grandfather Taught Me	112
The Good, The Bad, and The In-Between	118
Mr. Lonely, Pastrami on Rye, and a Life of Character	123
Briefs, Boxers, and Bad Men with Canes	127
Peppered Moths, Flying Finns, and Uncle Joe Meets His Maker	132
Man Caves, Modern Art, and Suckers	136
Beer, Milk Bone Underwear, and Higher Education	140
Down and QWERTY	145
Dancing Like Tigger and Snorting Coins Out My Nose	151
Lightning Bolts in the Hands of Zeus	154
Would You Like Your Naughty Boy Pie With Ice Cream or Cheese?	158
Cutting the Mustard Before The Reaper Drops In	164
What I Learned From Rod Serling	168
Scammers, Snake Oil Salesmen, and O. J. Simpson	173
Edison Medicine and the Hitchhiker from Hell	179
On Melting Down	184
Time, Tide, and Two Dead Trees	190
You Can Scarf Dogs But You Can't Fake Cool	196
A Duke, Pansy O'Hara, and Garbo's Feet	200
Me, Boone's Farm Apple Wine, and My Best Friend Randy	205
More Buns!	211
About James Scott Bell	213

RUNNING WITH THE WHITE RABBIT

Alice was beginning to get very tired of sitting by her sister on the bank, and of having nothing to do... when suddenly a White Rabbit with pink eyes ran close by her.

There was nothing so very remarkable in that; nor did Alice think it so very much out of the way to hear the Rabbit say to itself, "Oh dear! Oh dear! I shall be late!"... but when the Rabbit actually took a watch out of its waistcoat-pocket, and looked at it, and then hurried on, Alice started to her feet, for it flashed across her mind that she had never before seen a rabbit with either a waistcoat-pocket, or a watch to take out of it, and burning with curiosity, she ran across the field after it, and fortunately was just in time to see it pop down a large rabbit-hole under the hedge.

In another moment down went Alice after it, never once considering how in the world she was to get out again. (*Alice's Adventures in Wonderland* by Lewis Carroll.)

Good on you, Alice! Dive down rabbit holes, even though you don't know what you'll find!

The White Rabbit, we are told by scholars, represents "curiosity's pull and the entry into the absurd." And Alice is "the innocent pursuit of the unknown."

Which is just what my "Whimsical Wanderings" are all about. Some years ago I wrote a book called *Some People Are Dead: Part Essay, Part Memoir, Parts Unknown*. These were riffs off a random obituary, following whatever thoughts occurred, all the way to some delightful end. It found an appreciative readership:

> "I'm not sure how one would classify the genre of this book. There really aren't any like it. Perhaps the closest is the Meditations of Marcus Aurelius. I've reread this book a couple of times ... I find it to be a book that I can turn to just for a moment of decompression, and often for an insight that allows me to see one of my own challenges from a new perspective."

> "I read this in the hospital while recovering from surgery! Like a professor who seems to ramble and then pulls everything together into something profound, there is wisdom in this book. Life lessons, humor, quiet observations, smiles."

> "The wit of Vonnegut with a faithful thread of joy running through it. It had me laughing and crying in spots."

So here is more of the same. (I've since added random words from the dictionary to the White Rabbit's tail.) There's a definite purpose in this. I want these pieces to provide quick relief in this mad, mad world, a respite from all the ranting and raving and click-bait vitriol.

This collection of contemplations, musings, reflections, ruminations, meditations, broodings, and reveries (and the value of a Thesaurus!) are best dipped into when you need a break from the news, social media, waiting in line, and commercials for some pharmaceutical breakthrough, you know the kind: *If your partner keeps you up at night, ask your doctor about Snorvexa. May cause hacking, wheezing, levitation, or growing a third eye.*

Come and enjoy running after the White Rabbit with me, where each step is a doozy, and each hole a world of its own—and not so random as you might think!

Jim

DO NOT GO HATLESS INTO THAT GOOD NIGHT

I open the dictionary at random and find this word: *Epithelium*.

This is a word I was not familiar with, or with which I was not familiar (for classic grammarians out there) so I read the definition, to wit: *A membranous tissue composed of one or more layers of cells which forms the covering of most internal and external surfaces of the body and its organs.* Which, it seems to me, makes epithelia pretty important, sort of like clothes if you're going in for a job interview, in which case it's best to have clothes on covering most of your internal and external surfaces.

There used to be a saying, "Clothes make the man," which was a way of stating that how a man dresses in the sphere of business has something to do with increasing the odds of his success. Why is there no analogue for women, i.e., "Clothes make the woman," when a nicely dressed woman is just as important in the realm of business as a man, and it is the women who have fashion shows and models walking the runway, doing what is called a "catwalk" which is not an easy thing to do as there are several parts of the body to get right, like shoulders (back), hips (forward), face (relaxed), feet (straight line), kidneys (in place), and membranous tissue covering all organs?

And as far as women's clothing goes, I miss the era of women's hats and milliners (those who practice millinery, which is the making of women's hats, so called because a trade in fine hats arose in the city of Milan in the Middle Ages because the place was the hub of the world's textile and fashion trade. Those who made hats for men were called merely "hatters," not very original, which no doubt drove some of them mad).

When you watch movies from the 1930s and 40s, you'll see a lot of women's hats, and then on episodic TV from the 1950s, like *Perry Mason*, where a woman testifying in court would often wear a hat. The whole era of hats started to come to an end with the election of John Fitzgerald Kennedy as President of the United States. He went outside without a hat, unlike his predecessor Dwight David Eisenhower, and because JFK was young and vibrant, as opposed to DDE, who was more like your golfing grandfather, men who wanted to appear young and vibrant started not wearing hats, and though JFK's wife, Jackie, often wore a hat, and the Queen of England always wore a hat, the women's hat industry also began to decline, and the era of hippies arose, where women just let their hair grow down and straight. No more trips to the "beauty parlor" as they put it in those days.

And I ask you to consider with me whether or not society is better off without hats. Are we more civil to each other? Is there more or less order in our cities? You see, when Jack Webb as Joe Friday wore fedoras in the 1950s *Dragnet* TV show, law and order were pretty much in place. When the show came back in the 60s, Joe Friday was hatless, and where has that gotten us? Have you been to Los Angeles lately? All that to say, membranous tissue is a crucial covering for our internal organs, and hats may well be a crucial covering for our heads, and perhaps we'd better think all that through again.

"Without hats there is no civilization." – Christian Dior

"In that direction," the Cat said, waving its right paw round, "lives a Hatter: and in that direction," waving the other paw, "lives a March Hare. Visit either you like: they're both mad."

"But I don't want to go among mad people," Alice remarked.

"Oh, you can't help that," said the Cat: "we're all mad here. I'm mad. You're mad."

"How do you know I'm mad?" said Alice.

"You must be," said the Cat, "or you wouldn't have come here." – Lewis Carroll, *Alice's Adventures in Wonderland*

FOR A HEALTHY MARRIAGE, DON'T BE THIS

Dorothy Norcross died at the age of 101. Her obit indicates she had a good, full life, and was married to her college sweetheart, Claude, for 70 years. Seventy! That's the biblical span of life—"three score years and ten." People married young seventy years and more ago, with the expectation that they'd stay together until "death do you part." Claude and Dorothy made that pledge and stuck to it.

For thirty of those years Dorothy was an elementary school teacher. This was back in the era when teachers were conscientious, trusted, diligent, well-groomed, and mature. I actually remember those days.

I had a young teacher in sixth grade named Mrs. Greenberg. I could tell she loved her job. She enjoyed seeing little eyes light up with new understandings. Looking back, I would guess she was about 23 years old. I hope she and Mr. Greenberg made it to fifty years, at least.

In that class was a girl named Susan, who had red hair and green eyes, which drew me in, but she not interested in my eyes or anything else about me, so the main thing I learned in Mrs. Greenberg's class was how to take rejection—not very well. This was my second rejection from a girl named Susan in elementary school. In third grade it had happened, too, with a blonde-haired, blue-eyed Susan. I resolved not to fall for any more Susans, or Sues, or Susies after I left elementary school. Thankfully, we have a full alphabet. I dated an Alicia. I never dated a Zenobia.

The classical word for teaching is *pedagogy*. This is from two Greek words: *Pedo* (child) and *agogos* (leader). The latter word is not to be confused with A-Go-Go, which came into fashion in the 1960s on the Sunset Strip in L.A. There was a nightclub called The Whisky A-Go-Go. It was a venue for rock. The Doors, with Jim Morrison, got their start there, and a singer with Big Brother and the Holding Company named Janis Joplin.

Joplin and Morrison both died of heroin overdoses at the age of 27. Jimi Hendrix died of barbiturate OD at 27. Later, Kurt Cobain of Nirvana OD'd at 27, giving rise to an urban myth called "The 27 Club" which holds that there's a spike in celebrity deaths at 27 years of age.

I made it past 27, maybe because I wasn't a celebrity. I was an actor, though, whose genius was undiscovered. I'd been in productions of both *Hamlet* and *Othello*, the former in Hollywood and the latter in New York. In *Hamlet* I played Rosencrantz, a small but vital character. Along with Guildenstern, he tries to find out what's going on with his friend Hamlet at the behest of King Claudius. He's a suck-up to the king and a sneak (snake?) with Hamlet.

Well, I was so good in that part that I got a one-line notice in a trade review. "James Scott Bell is nicely oily as Rosencrantz." There you have it! Nicely oily! What an item to put on my résumé! (Although, after I became a lawyer, maybe that notice would have recommended me to a law firm.)

I was 27 the year I got married. My wife and I have been together 44 years. It's till death do us part, like it was for Dorothy and Claude. The secret to a good marriage? The man should *not* to be nicely oily.

Definition of Alimony: Bounty on the mutiny. – Evan Esar

HARPOONS AND HEMORRHOIDS

Random word: *Harpooner*.

You don't hear much about harpooners these days. It's a lost art, the throwing of a spear-like projectile into the blubber of a whale. We don't need whale oil anymore, so let's leave the majestic mammals alone to swim around and have calves and spout water.

But in the old whaling days, the ability to harpoon was highly valued, as demonstrated by Melville's character Queequeg, the tattooed harpoon thrower who befriends Ishmael, only after he finds Ishmael in his bed.

Have you ever come home and found a stranger asleep in your bed? It would be a might disconcerting. Queequeg almost impales Ishmael, but then becomes his friend, but then proves to be gentle as a kitten. Phew.

Harpoons are still used by whaling nations, but now they're shot out of a gun or cannon, which seems the height of unfairness. At least when it was a throwing competition the whale had a chance.

There is another use of the word "whale" and that is when it refers to a high roller, a fabulously wealthy individual who doesn't mind throwing his money around, usually by gambling, which makes casino operators like harpooners, trying to land these players and make it attractive for them to spend all that dough in their gambling dens.

I was never a whale when I went to Las Vegas with my college roommates. We were guppies swimming around with barracudas, preserving our meager stakes by playing blackjack at the cheapest tables. I recall with embarrassment going into a place with my roomie, Rick, sitting at a table and placing a bet with a fifty cent chip. "It's a dollar here, fellas," the dealer said. A whole dollar! So, like brave and intrepid adventurers, we meekly took back our chips and slunk out of there. Suffice to say, no casino made any effort to harpoon us.

I'm not a gambler anymore, except when it comes to Pascal's Wager. I've placed my bet on there being something rather than nothing after death.

From my grandfather's Encyclopedia Britannica set: *Harpoon* is on the same page as *Harpsichord* and *Harpies*. Of the harpsichord: "What these instruments gain in brilliancy of tone, however, they lose in power of expression and of accent."

Harpies are found in the legend of Jason and the Argonauts, webby-winged creatures with "the faces of women, horribly foul and loathsome." They are sent to torment a blind man named Phineus for some offense against the gods, and do so by nearly starving him to death by carrying off most of his food and "befouling the rest." In the movie, Jason and his men capture the harpies, who are brought to screen life by the legendary special effects man, Ray Harryhausen, a childhood friend of Ray Bradbury.

Turning the page in my grandfather's Encyclopedia Britannica I find the word *Hemorrhoids*. I did not plan this, I promise you. The article informs me that these are commonly called piles, and are "swellings formed by the dilation of veins of the lowest part of the bowel, or just outside the margin of its aperture."

It actually triggers a memory. The great Hall of Fame baseball player George Brett, of the Kansas City Royals, once had to have hemorrhoid surgery. When he came back he was asked by a TV reporter how he felt. Brett replied, "My problems are all behind me now." I'm sure he'd been planning that one for a while, which proves once again that most humor comes out of pain. "If it bends, it's comedy. If it breaks, it's tragedy." So says the obnoxious but highly successful producer played by Alan Alda in Woody Allen's *Crimes and Misdemeanors*.

There's a biblical account of piles from the 1 Samuel in the Bible, when the Philistines captured the Ark of the Covenant. Instead of avenging spirits shooting out to melt their faces, God instead afflicted them with "emerods" and I'm sure after a few days of that the Philistines would have preferred to have their faces melted. So they sent the Ark to Gath, the hometown of Goliath, but the men of Gath got emerods, too, "in their secret parts."

Finally, the Philistine priests said, "Idiots! Send it back! And with an offering." So they sent it back by cart, with five gold emerods as an offering. Now how is that for a goldsmith's trade? "Hey Harry, take a look at this. Can you make five of these out of gold?"

The usual palliative for piles, says the encyclopedia, is "obtaining an easy and daily action of..." —I'm not going to go into it—"and cold bathing, astringent injections, lotions and ointments." If those don't work, an operation is called for. "The usual operation consists in strangling the pile by ligatures."

Now, aren't you glad you're reading this book? I thank you for your kind attention.

"Friendship, like love, is destroyed by long absence, though it may be increased by short intermissions." – Samuel Johnson

HARMONICAS AND HUSBANDS

Richard Chamberlain died at the age of 90. He was at one time a teen heartthrob, starring in the TV show *Dr. Kildare*. I remember one girl in my elementary school who had a Dr. Kildare lunch pail. I had Zorro on mine.

I respected Chamberlain for his dedication to his craft. After *Dr. Kildare* ended, he went to England to study. He returned as a fine stage actor and "the king of the miniseries," such as *The Thorn Birds* and *Shogun*. He had a prosperous career and acted well into his 80s.

He also had a brother, Bill, who coached me in Little League. Bill was even more handsome than Richard. Good genes in that family.

Once, Bill asked me if I wanted to be a baseball player when I grew up. I said, "No, I want to be a lover."

He howled with laughter. "I'm with you!"

I was all of twelve years old. But I dug Errol Flynn, especially in *The Adventures of Robin Hood* (1938), and wanted to woo a maid as beautiful as Olivia de Havilland. (Later I got that chance, and married the girl. That was 44 years ago and I'm still in love.)

Flynn himself was a fine actor, but a notorious rake offscreen. He lost a step or two after the war, though he's still in good form in *The Adventures of Don Juan* (1948).

In the 1950s, puffy from drink, he could still act, and is superb in a supporting role in *The Sun Also Rises* (1957). A proposed sequel about a humble baker, *The Dough Also Rises*, was never made.

There are other things that should never be made. Beet juice, a remake of *Casablanca* or a sequel to *Gone With the Wind* (there was an attempt at this, in the 1990s, but I never read it. I've heard it's about Scarlett going into the window drapes business, then finding Rhett in Charleston performing with a musical troupe called The Harmonica Rascals).

Speaking of harmonicas (and I was), they are played by breath, putting it among the bravest of all musical instruments, for it can withstand the stink of garlic, onions, sardines, cheap cigars, hot sauce and gastric juices. It laughs at halitosis. It fears not gingivitis.

Its origins can be traced back to ancient China and an instrument called the *sheng* (trans: vibrating reed thingy). The Germans took it over (as they are wont to do) and developed the modern mouth organ in the early 1800s. It came over to America and was popular during the Civil War, around campfires, helping to drown out the sounds made after a meal of beans and bacon. (Remember that campfire scene in *Blazing Saddles*? That was actually documentary footage.)

The harmonica also made its way into prison movies, usually as some guy was about to be marched off to the electric chair. I will not repeat the joke about the guy who bought his mother-in-law a chair, and complained that she won't plug it in. That would be distasteful. To be fair, there are plenty of husband jokes, too, e.g.,

"I have a model husband. He's just not a working model."

There are many poems and books about love and romance, but not many about marriage. We all know that marriage has its challenges. I like to imagine what might have happened if Jack had survived the sinking of the *Titanic*. A year later Rose would be saying, "Will you go out and get a job already? And stop sketching me as I get out of the shower! And if I catch you gambling again, you're out on your ear!"

See, I'm a romantic at heart.

Being "out on your ear" is slang of unknown origin, though we find it being well-used in the early 20th century. It may have had something to do with pratfall in Vaudeville. It's a funny and ignominious way to land.

People used to say "Keep your ear to the ground," which means be alert to things going on around you, things that might indicate change or trouble coming. They also used to say, "Keep your nose to the grindstone." Impossible! Have you ever tried keeping your nose to the grindstone with your ear on the ground?

"Ear of corn," by the way, has nothing to do with the canals on the sides of our head, the word *ear* deriving from an Old English word for *husk*.

Which brings up the phrase, "He's a husk of his former self," which is something you never want to be. So keep your mind vibrant and curious, and do what you can to maintain a healthy husk. Clint Eastwood has a healthy husk, at age 94. Once, singer Toby Keith asked him how he keeps going, and Eastwood replied:

Every day when I wake up, I don't let the old man in. My secret has been the same since 1959—staying busy. I never let the old man into the house. I've had to drag him out because he was already comfortably settled, bothering me all the time, leaving no space for anything other than nostalgia.

You have to stay active, alive, happy, strong, and capable. It's in us, in our intelligence, attitude, and mentality. We are young, regardless of our ID. We must learn to fight to not let the old man in.

That's a fight worth having. Winston Churchill was 65 when he became Prime Minister of England at the beginning of World War II. He'd had a colorful life, with plenty of ups and downs. In his magnificent history of the war, he recounts the moment he assumed power. "I felt as if I were walking with destiny, and that all my past life had been but a preparation for this hour and for this trial."

Your life has prepped you, too. This is your moment.

"The hardest years in life are those between ten and seventy." – Legendary Broadway actress Helen Hayes at age 83

EINSTEIN'S BOX TOP AND DIMAGGIO'S DISAPPEARANCE

Stephanie Miller Asker, a pioneer in women's psychotherapy, died at the age of 91. Her obit notes that she was one of the last living persons to know Albert Einstein. Her father, a CPA, became Einstein's accountant and friend. Stephanie met the great man when she was four, and would often visit his home in New Jersey along with her parents.

When she was nine she asked Einstein about his theory of relativity. He promised to explain it to her when she was older.

She reminded him of the promise when she was twelve. So he took the top of a cake box and drew on it illustrations of a train station and an elevator...and wouldn't you love to have that box top? I still wouldn't understand the theory, but I'd have one heckuva conversation piece for my wall.

Which is why people collect autographs, of course. Little pieces of scribbled celebrity that sometimes gain value over time. In fact, a 1946 autographed photo of Einstein is one of the most valuable of such items, at around ten grand, because Al wasn't exactly loose with his pen.

Abraham Lincoln signed 48 copies of the Emancipation Proclamation, half of which are lost. One of the remaining copies sold at auction for $2.1 million back in 2012. That seems about right. You would not expect to spend that much on a Millard Fillmore or a James K. Polk, but for Honest Abe, yes.

And you'd think that John Hancock's John Hancock would be the most valuable among the signers of the Declaration of Independence. But that honor actually belongs to a more obscure rebel named Button Gwinnett. A 1770s document with his signature went for nearly $722,500 back in 2010.

Gwinnett, by the way, was not given his first name because his mother thought him "cute as a button" when he was born (and where did that idiom come from, anyway? What is so cute about a button? "Sturdy as a button" maybe, if you have a pair of stud-fly Levis. But cute? Apparently, in merry old England where the phrase comes from, a button refers to a flower bud, which makes more sense. But I still can't make head or tail out of "cute as a bug's ear"), but rather because he was named in honor of his mother's cousin, Barbara Button, of the Gloucester Buttons, who fastened themselves to high society (see what I did there? This is why you read Whimsical Wanderings).

Other valuable signatures are Jimmy Page's autographed Gibson guitar and a baseball signed by that fun couple, Joe DiMaggio and Marilyn Monroe.

I was too young to have seen DiMaggio play, but his name was well known to us Boomers, and not just for baseball. He was for many years the TV pitchman for Mr. Coffee, and he's also a lyric in the Simon and Garfunkel song "Mrs. Robinson." That song was part of the score for the movie *The Graduate* (1967), starring Dustin Hoffman as the

CINNAMON BUNS AND MILK BONE UNDERWEAR

titular character, and the brilliant Anne Bancroft as Mrs. Robinson.

Where have you gone, Joe DiMaggio? the song asks. I have a sneaking suspicion Paul Simon chose that name because it scanned well, sounded good. As opposed to, say, *Where have you gone, Fred Flintsone?*

Joltin' Joe has left and gone away, the song answers. It became a huge hit.

Some years later, in a New York restaurant, Simon was introduced to Joe DiMaggio, who said to him, "What I don't understand is why you ask where I've gone. I just did a Mr. Coffee commercial."

Simon thought fast and said he used Mr. DiMaggio as a symbol for old-fashioned values and heroism, gone now from a cynical society.

What Simon didn't tell Joltin' Joe (aka, The Yankee Clipper) was that he was really a fan of DiMaggio's replacement, Mickey Mantle. But Mickey's name also didn't scan as well for the song. Try it. Thud.

Speaking of The Mick, Jim Bouton was a Yankees pitcher in the 1960s who wrote the first tell-all book about baseball, *Ball Four*. In there he has a story about Mantle, who liked to hoist a few. He came in one day for a game, completely hung over. The manager told him to sleep it off, they'd put somebody else in center field.

But the game went into extra innings and the Yankees needed a pinch hitter. So they grabbed Mickey off the table. He went to the plate, took a practice swing, then smashed a towering home run into the bleachers.

He somehow made it around the bases but missed home plate. Some players hustled him back to touch it.

In the dugout, a player asked him how he hit a homer in his condition. Mantle said, "I hit the middle ball."

JAMES SCOTT BELL

~

"Be brief, for no discourse can please when too long." – Cervantes

A poem by an anonymous Scottish poet from 150 years ago:

> He was a burglar stout and strong,
> Who held, "It surely can't be wrong
> To open trunks and rifle shelves,
> For God helps those who help themselves."
> But when before the Court he came,
> And boldly rose to plead the same,
> The judge replied: "That's very true;
> You've helped yourself—now God help you!"

CINNAMON BUNS, WILT THE STILT, AND BILL WALTON'S BEARD

Mary Carole Lynch died at the age of 91. Her obituary describes her as a "woman of deep faith and tireless hands." She loved cooking, could bake a pie "for any occasion," and was known for her "legendary" sticky cinnamon rolls. She and her husband of 67 years lived on a farm, so those rolls would have been made from scratch and didn't cheat you on the size.

I've eaten many a cinnamon bun, but I can't say I've ever met a legend. I've met famous people, even passed some on the street, like Wilt Chamberlain, who I saw on a corner in New York City one night. Chamberlain was 7′1″ and the first truly dominant big man in the history of basketball (apologies to George Mikan of the Minneapolis Lakers...yes, the Los Angeles Lakers started in Minneapolis, which is why they are called the *Lakers* and not the *Freeways*. And the Los Angeles Dodgers got their name because they started in Brooklyn, and to get to Ebbets Field you had to walk across busy trolley tracks, leading to their nickname, the Trolley Dodgers. I'm not making this up).

One season "Wilt the Stilt" averaged—*averaged*—fifty points a game! He's the only player ever to score 100 points in a single game even though he couldn't shoot free throws worth a darn. (When he started, players were allowed to jump past the free throw line, and Wilt would take a running start, leap like a gazelle, and dunk the ball! The NBA changed that rule right quick.)

Wilt's physical strength was prodigious and he set records for rebounding. Off the court, he apparently tried to set another kind of record. He once told an interviewer he'd had intimate relations with 20,000 women. A journalist calculated this out, and it amounted to 1.22 partners per day, every day, for 45 years. That didn't leave much time for basketball practice.

And by the way, practice does not make perfect. *Perfect* practice makes perfect. You can practice something all you want in the wrong way and ingrain only deleterious muscle memory. I can practice hitting piano keys all day long, but I will never tickle the ivories like Chico Marx. I took exactly one piano lesson, when I was in high school, from the wife of my math teacher who lived down the street from me. I learned where Middle C was and how to play a simple number called "Mr. Frog Is Full of Hops." I don't remember why I stopped the lessons, but I suppose it had something to do with the practice demands of basketball.

And if I may, I find basketball unwatchable now. It's been ruined by the three-point shot and analytics. Not like the glory days of college basketball, when UCLA was the dominant power and John Wooden the head coach, and the Bruins ran plays and strategized and had an awesome full-court press. John Wooden was a true legend, and I got to talk to him because I went to the John Wooden Basketball Camp one summer in high school. One day I was outside the gym and there was John Wooden himself changing a tire on his car. Changing a tire? Legends change tires? I offered to help and he said no thanks, he was just putting the hubcap back on. I remember distinctly he was sitting on the asphalt and he kicked the hubcap with the bottom of his foot to secure it. He was probably 64 years old at the time, and I remember thinking how athletic that kick was. Of course! Wooden was a three-time All American basketball player at Purdue.

He was also a man of faith with rock solid principles, as Bill Walton found out.

One of Wooden's star players in the 1970s, Walton was embracing the "free spirit" vibe of the time and showed up for fall basketball practice with a scraggly beard, even though Wooden had a policy requiring players to be clean-shaven.

Wooden calmly remarked, "Bill, have you forgotten something?"

"Coach," Walton replied, "I'm allowed to express my individuality."

"That's fine, Bill," Wooden said. "I admire your independence. We're going to miss you."

Walton went straight to the locker room and shaved off his beard. I have no doubt at all that Wooden would have kicked Walton off the team, even though it probably would have meant losing a national title.

Andy Roddick was one of America's great tennis players. In 2005 he had a match against a Spanish player, Fernando Verdasco, in Italy. Roddick was the #1 seed.

At triple match point, all Roddick had to do was break Verdasco's serve to win it all. Verdasco's first serve was a fault. His second serve was a monster and Roddick couldn't reach it. But the linesman called it out.

The crowd cheered, and Verdasco ran to the net to congratulate Roddick. But Roddick went to the umpire and told him the serve had hit the line. He went over and pointed to the mark on the clay where the ball had hit. The umpire reversed the call and awarded the point to Verdasco.

And then the seemingly impossible happened. Verdasco won that game, went on to win the set and the match.

A famous sportswriter named Frank DeFord estimated that Roddick's honesty cost him at least "tens of thousands of dollars."

Championships are worth something, but integrity is priceless.

~

"If I were two-faced, would I be wearing this one?" – Abraham Lincoln

OF BASEBALL, BRONX, AND BLUSTER

Cynthia Ann Egan died in The Bronx at the age of 88. She grew up, got educated, got married, lived and died in The Bronx. That's quite an achievement. One doesn't usually associate long life with certain boroughs of New York.

The Bronx gets its name from one Jonas Bronck, who may have been Swedish. He came to America in 1639 and settled in New Amsterdam, which is what they called New York City in those days. There wasn't a decent delicatessen anywhere, which got Bronck to thinking that maybe food services wasn't the business for him.

He looked across what has come to be called the East River, and said to himself, "One day, this mighty river will be filled with boats and ferries and Teamsters with cement shoes, and on the other side prime real estate, which I shall snap up."

So he purchased a big swath of land, which also had a river, which they started calling The Bronck's River or, simply, The Broncks. A lazy map maker discovered he could shave a second or two off his duties by dropping the cks and replacing it with an x.

A mighty baseball team arose called "The Bronx Bombers" because they played their games in Yankee Stadium which, by a wild coincidence, was their team name —the New York Stadiums. When they got Babe Ruth, he suggested they change the name to the Bambinos. They settled on Yankees so they wouldn't have to change the name on the stadium.

Babe Ruth was sometimes called The Sultan of Swat or The Colossus of Clout. He could have been called the Downer of Dogs for his prodigious appetite that once chomped 16 hot dogs before a game. He hit 714 career home run and one can only imagine what he could have done had he kept his body in shape like his teammate, Lou Gehrig.

Life being the unfair contest that it is, Gehrig's body was felled by the horrible ALS. Before that, Gehrig's nickname was The Iron Horse, because he never missed a game after taking over for First Baseman Wally Pipp in 1925. His record of 2,130 consecutive games was thought to be unbreakable until Cal Ripkin came along and made it to 2,632.

The current "never to be broken" baseball record is Joe DiMaggio's 56 game hitting streak. That broke the record of 45 in 1896, set by "Wee" Willie Keeler, whose philosophy was "Hit 'em where they ain't."

The closest anyone has come since is Pete Rose's 44 game streak. Rose holds the major league record for career hits and yet is not in the Hall of Fame. He had placed bets on baseball games (never on his own team to lose) and then lied about it.

Pete Rose died without getting his rightful place in the Baseball Hall of Fame. Many an off-field sinner is in the Hall, which should judge a player by what he does on the field.

No one played the game with more reckless abandon

than Pete Rose. When he got a walk he never sauntered to first base. He ran as if he was beating out a grounder.

The Holy Writ against betting on baseball was chiseled by the hardscrabble commissioner Kenesaw Mountain Landis, after what is known as the "Black Sox scandal." A few players on the Chicago White Sox took money from gamblers to "fix" the 1919 World Series.

One of the players implicated was Joe Jackson, nicknamed "Shoeless Joe," who was one of the top three hitters ever to play the game (along with Ty Cobb and Rogers Hornsby). He was a simple country boy who probably didn't fully grasp what was going on with the money changing hands. Even though he performed masterfully in the Series, hitting .375, he was indicted for fraud along with seven teammates and five gamblers.

And even though the jury came back with a verdict of not guilty, Landis banned all the players for life.

A famous (though probably apocryphal) story has it that when Jackson came out of the courtroom, a little boy ran up to him with tears streaming down his face. "Say it ain't so, Joe!" the tyke said.

"I'm afraid it is," said Joe.

Many years later Joe Jackson was running a liquor store in his home town of Greenville, South Carolina. One day the greatest hitter of all, Ty Cobb, came in. Jackson said nothing. Cobb approached him and said, "What's the matter, Joe? Don't you remember me?"

Jackson replied, "Sure I do, Ty. I just didn't think you wanted me to."

Shoeless Joe got a small measure of redemption when he came out of the cornfield in *Field of Dreams*, the Kevin Costner movie, and got to play baseball again.

Random noun: *bluster*.

We do have abundant bluster in our favored land. From politics to sports to media, the sound of self-aggrandizement fills the air, spawning yet more of the same, stomping all over the rare jewel of humility.

Stanley Kowalski in *A Streetcar Named Desire* is all bluster and uses it to stomp all over his sister-in-law, Blanche DuBois:

Blanche: Oh, in my youth I excited some admiration. But look at me now! Would you think it possible that I was once considered to be attractive?

Stanley: Your looks is okay.

Blanche: I was fishing for a compliment, Stanley.

Stanley: I don't go in for that stuff.

Blanche: What stuff?

Stanley: Compliments to women about their looks. I never met a dame yet didn't know she was good lookin' or not without bein' told, and some of them give themselves credit for more than they got. I once went out with a dame who told me, "I'm the glamorous type," she says. "I am the glamorous type." I says, "So what?"

Blanche: And what did she say then?

Stanley: She didn't say nothin'. That shut her up like a clam.

Blanche: Did it end the romance?

Stanley: Well, it ended the conversation, that was all.

Here's an anonymous poem published in an L.A. periodical, December, 1920:

I love to watch a rooster crow.
He's like so many men I know,
Who brag and bluster, ramp and shout,
And beat their manly chests without
A single thing to crow about.

TROUPERS, LOVERS, AND AUNT BEBE'S BEAN BOWL

Glynis Johns died at the age of 100. She was best known as Mrs. Banks in the 1964 Disney movie *Mary Poppins*. She had a perky personality and a sandpaper voice that I would describe as "cute."

There are actresses who shoot to fame with beauty—Rita Hayworth comes to mind—and others who make it by way of sheer acting ability, like Jane Darwell, who was also in *Mary Poppins* as the lady who fed the birds. She was in many other fine films, including *The Grapes of Wrath*, for which she won the Best Supporting Actress Oscar.

Glynis Johns made it on acting ability and that voice, a voice that was the first to sing the timeless song "Send in the Clowns." She originated the role of Desiree Armfeld in Stephen Sondheim's *A Little Night Music*, for which she won a Tony.

She knew "Send in the Clowns" was going to be a standard, but when she was rushed to the hospital for an intestinal infection a few days before the show opened, there was concern about her being able to make it. Tammy Grimes

—another actress with a sandpaper voice, who had a daughter with Christopher Plummer named Amanda (who would later show up in Quentin Tarantino's *Pulp Fiction*, and who I met once at a party for actors in New York) was contacted to replace Glynis. When Glynis found out, she checked herself out of the hospital and played opening night, later saying, "I wasn't going to have anyone else sing my songs!"

That, in theatre parlance, is a "Trouper" (not "Trooper") from the old word for acting troupe—traveling actors who often had to perform under adversity. There's no compliment an actor prizes more than being thought of as a trouper. Good on Glynis for a long and trouping career.

In a random obituary, I see that Peggy J. Gordon died. Her obit says she was a woman who "worked hard and loved extravagantly." Isn't that the best way to work and the best way to love? When you work, put all your effort into it. Do your best and leave it all out there on the field, as the football coaches like to say.

And when you love, let it be extravagant! Let it be a Beethoven symphony, a choir of angels singing Ode to Joy!

I've personally known only two Peggys in my life. One was a neighbor girl who lived around the corner. The other was a nice older woman who attended the same church as I and seemed the most like a Peggy. And what is that? I imagine like the character Peggotty in *David Copperfield*, the housekeeper who befriends and comforts little David. Later she becomes the object of affection for the coach driver, Mr. Barkis, who is too shy to ask her to marry him, so tells David to give her a message: "Barkis is willin'." The two do get married, and in their own way it is an extravagant love, for that is possible for anyone regardless of station in life.

Of course, to love extravagantly is also to risk having one's heart stomped on, bringing to mind the old saying, "Tis better to have loved and had your heart stomped on than never to have loved at all."

Was it better that I loved Susan in third grade? And that I worked up the courage to walk next to her on the way home, and that she turned to me and said, derisively, "Just because I'm letting you walk with me doesn't mean you're my boyfriend!"

The way she said boyfriend was like a stake through the heart, like she was Van Helsing and I was Dracula, when all I wanted to be was Robin Hood to her Maid Marion.

I just remembered another Peggy, the English actress Peggy Ashcroft, who has an unforgettable bit in Alfred Hitchcock's *The 39 Steps* (1935). She helps the fleeing Robert Donat, even though her harsh Scottish (and considerably older) husband suspects her romantic interest in him. After she helps Donat escape, we are left with the impression that her husband is going to do some Scottish rock-soil hammering on her.

Dame Peggy went on to a long and distinguished stage career, specializing in Shakespeare. She received an Academy Award nomination for Best Supporting Actress in David Lean's *A Passage to India* (1984).

The only other Peggy from my memory was just a Peg, Peg Bracken, a humor writer in the 1960s who wrote a book my mom had (and laughed at) called *The I Hate to Cook Book*. It acknowledged that not every "housewife" was into prepping extravagant meals. Here were recipes that were simple to throw together and had funny names, like "Clam Whiffle" and "Spuds O'Grotten" (supposedly named for "Mother O'Grotten" who emigrated from County Cork. See? Funny).

My wife, Cindy, whom I love extravagantly, brought her own copy into our marriage, and I recently took it off the shelf for another look, and am ready to try some of the recipes myself. I think I'll start with "Aunt Bebe's Bean Bowl."

So the lesson here is that your love should be extravagant but your meals don't have to be. Unless you love to cook, in which case go for the Duck à l'orange anytime you like.

A Word to Husbands
by Ogden Nash

To keep your marriage brimming,
With love in the loving cup,
Whenever you're wrong, admit it;
Whenever you're right, shut up.

CHEWING GUM, THE GUMM SISTERS, AND GUMMING UP THE WORKS

Random word: *Gum*.

Ah, gum, thou sweet, malleable mouth magnificence. How much time in my youth did I spend in thy company? Why did not all my teeth rot?

There were three types of chewing gum favored by my young self.

First on the list was Bazooka, which came with a comic strip featuring Bazooka Joe and his "gang." And a little one- or two-line "fortune." In the 1950s, these "predictions" were likely to be grandiose, reflecting the optimism of the age, as in:

You are destined to have great riches and honor, mainly because of the fine power of your thinking.

By the 1980s, however, the fortunes had become more modest:

You will soon receive some good news.

CINNAMON BUNS AND MILK BONE UNDERWEAR

To have friends, first be a friend.
Take time to set a goal today.

The past few years have seen a further evolution:

Don't even think about trying. You'll never make it.
We're doomed, so drink as much as you want.

Then there was the stick of gum that came with baseball cards. This was a hard, powdery strip that cracked upon first contact with the mouth and had to be worked considerably to get into chewable form. This gum was masticated mainly because it was just there with the cards, not so much for taste. Looking at who you got in the cards distracted you from the hard chew experience. Among miscreants this gum quickly found its way to the underside of a desk.

And then there was Juicy Fruit. Ah, Juicy Fruit! Developed by the Wrigley company back in 1893. Wrigley was known mostly for Spearmint, which I could take or leave. But Juicy Fruit was an adventure. It was a jungle cruise down the Amazon. A sky dive over the Grand Canyon.

Juicy Fruit is the gum that finally gets Chief Broom to talk in the movie version of *One Flew Over the Cuckoo's Nest*. "Mm, Juicy Fruit," he says after taking a stick from McMurphy.

That's just the type of gum that could bring out the voice in a silent one.

In my visits to the corner liquor store and its candy section, I would buy a handful of Bazooka, a pack of Juicy Fruit, and some baseball cards. My other candy preferences were Good & Plenty, Necco Wafers, Three Musketeers, Baby Ruth, and U-No.

The U-No had this light center, like a truffle, not gooey

like a Mars bar. I felt like a seventeenth-century French king when I ate a U-No. It was not to be gobbled, but rolled around on the tongue.

I'm still waiting for a *Sleeper* moment for these tasties. In that Woody Allen movie a man wakes up in the future and is being brought up to speed by scientists. They smoke and eat fat and hot fudge sundaes, and tell him, "These were once thought to be unhealthy, precisely the opposite of what we now know to be true."

Which reminds me of Frances Ethel Gumm.

With her two sisters, Frances Gumm was part of a Vaudeville singing act known, unsurprisingly, as The Gumm Sisters. That was until a Vaudeville star, George Jessel, mentioned they were as pretty as a "garland of flowers" but deserved a more appealing name. Thus, Gumm became Garland, and Frances became Judy, one of the greatest entertainers of all time.

Signed at thirteen by MGM, she went on to make hugely popular musical comedies with Mickey Rooney, the classics *The Wizard of Oz* and *Meet Me in St. Louis*. Her acting chops were on display in her two Academy Award nominated performances—*A Star is Born* (1954) and *Judgment at Nuremberg* (1961).

The phrase "gumming up the works" goes back to the industrial revolution. Machines took over production and needed lubrication to run smoothly. If oil or something else congealed on the parts, the machine would sputter and the whole works brought to a halt. In the lumber business, tree sap was a culprit, as it could become a sticky wicket on the big saws.

The etymology of "sticky wicket" is beyond the scope of this article, except to say that it comes from the sport of Cricket, which no one understands, even the players.

Chew on that for a while.

"Your manuscript is both good and original; but the part that is good is not original, and the part that is original is not good." – Samuel Johnson

According to a 20-year study out of Johns Hopkins University, it has been shown that if your parents don't have children, you won't either.

THIS CHAPTER IS NOT MADE OF GENUINE FIBERGLAS

Joyce Randolph died at 99, and that is a fine age to be, a venerable age, a respected age, just shy of 100. She was an actress best known for playing Trixie on the old *Honeymooners* TV show.

In the show, Trixie was married to Ed Norton, played by Art Carney, who was often the foil for Ralph Kramden, played by Jackie Gleason. Ralph was married to the spunky Alice, played by Audrey Meadows, who gave as good as she got from Ralph, especially when he would get so mad he'd threaten to send her to the moon with his fist. She stood up to him with moxie and level-headedness. She is the true hero of the series.

Audrey Meadows' sister, Jayne, lived to be 95. She was married to Steve Allen, one of the greatest wits ever produced in America, or any other part of the world for that matter. He was the original host of *The Tonight Show* and was known for his quick, on-the-spot ad-libs, my favorite of which went like this: He often did live commercials on his show, and one was for Fiberglass...Steve was to take a hammer and bring it down on a Fiberglass chair. The hammer would bounce off, the chair would not budge, and the line after that was, "Yes, ladies and gentlemen, this chair is made of genuine Fiberglass."

Well, the studio was cold that night, and when it came time for the commercial—live, mind you—Steve Allen delivered the blow...and the chair cracked apart! Without missing a beat, Allen turned to the camera and said, "Yes, ladies and gentlemen, this hammer is made of genuine Fiberglass."

Steve Allen

There were many other legendary Steven Allen riffs and sketches. One sketch was set up as a movie trailer. Two cowboys are standing at a fence. The dialogue goes like this:

"I reckon there's gonna be trouble in town."
"I reckon you're right."

"I reckon we better take our guns."
"I reckon so."

Then the title of the movie splashes across the screen: DAY OF RECKONING.

Allen was a true Renaissance man. He wrote books…and songs! Lots and lots of songs, over eight thousand, and I can't even imagine being able to do that, primarily because I don't play the piano or carry tunes farther than the bathroom shower. But Allen did all of that, his most famous song being "This Could Be the Start of Something Big." It's still

Steve Allen got an obituary much too early (age 78) after a freak car accident which hurt his chest, but he didn't seek medical attention. As he slept, there was leakage of blood into the sac surrounding the heart due to a ruptured blood vessel. He never recovered.

Which brings me back to Joyce Randolph (don't as me how), who was not able to get any plum acting roles after *The Honeymooners* because she was "typecast" as Trixie, and that seems unfair, but it's how it went in those days, like George Reeves who was once a working character actor (in movies like *Gone With the Wind* and *From Here to Eternity*) and then got cast as TV's Superman, after which he couldn't get arrested as anybody else but Superman.

If there's a lesson to be learned in all this it's that you just never know how time and tide will treat you, so don't worry about it, don't let it keep you up at night, just go about your days, each day, putting your best self out there and letting the chips fall where they may…and if those happen to be potato chips, enjoy them.

"Without laughter life on our planet would be intolerable. So important is laughter to us that humanity highly rewards members of one of the most unusual professions on earth, those who make a living by inducing laughter in others. This is very strange if you stop to think of it: that otherwise sane and responsible citizens should devote their professional energies to causing others to make sharp, explosive barking-like exhalations." – Steve Allen

"I'm tired of all this nonsense about beauty being only skin-deep. That's deep enough. What do you want, an adorable pancreas?" – Jean Kerr

HONOR, DUTY, AND MONKEYSHINES

Harry E. Bridgett of Sioux City died, age 77. He was buried with military honors, which tells me he served in Vietnam. Anyone who was in that horror show deserves military honors. Indeed, anyone dutifully serving our country does.

I remember my grandfather's funeral. I was a teenager, and we gathered in the chapel at Hollywood Forever Cemetery, where "Padre" (Arthur Scott Bell, Sr.) worked late in his life as a salesman, which is what he was, selling Encyclopedia Britannica's during the Depression. He was in the Army in WWI, and because of his athletic prowess was put in charge of training soldiers stateside.

When an old V.A. fellow went to my grandmother with the folded flag that had been on Padre's coffin, and placed it in her hands saying, "This is very dear to us," I busted out crying.

Honor, duty—two words we need to say more, and mean them.

Manuel Gonzalez Sanchez of San Antonio died at the age of 81, survived by many Sanchezes, including eight great grandchildren. Growing up in SoCal and playing sports, I knew Sanchezes and Medinas and Mr. Padilla, who liked to give kids Mexican bread on Cinco de Mayo.

In elementary school we'd celebrate the holiday by dressing up in sombreros and serapes and listening to mariachi music and learning about the Spanish and Mexican roots of California, and you know what? No mob came screaming at us kids to knock it off. It was a much happier time, and friendlier.

I was friends with Joe Medina, played Little League with him. His parents ran a mom-and-pop Mexican restaurant on Ventura Boulevard called Casa Medina. The food was ample, and Señora Medina did most of the hostessing. The fresh, warm, homemade flour tortillas were to faint for, as dying was not an option if you wanted to keep eating at Casa Medina.

I've always loved Mexican food. And Italian and Chinese. Not so much French food, but I prefer it to British cuisine, if there is such a thing. I mean, blood pudding?

John Michael "Johnny" Robling died, in Idaho. He had three daughters, 9 grandchildren, and 7 great grandchildren, a cornucopia of family, a cup that runneth over.

The obit says, "He never met a stranger" because he always had something "exciting" to talk about. I presume it wasn't the weather or his corns that dominated his conversations, which is a good lesson for us all.

Will Rogers, the American humorist of the early 20th century, famously said, "I never met a man I didn't like."

Which has always puzzled me, because I have met some stink bombs in my time, and even tried to have a nice conversation with a few, only to find that odiousness stayed stuck to them like, as the saying goes, ugly on a frog. Indeed, I've met plenty of strangers; one of them tried to trap me in his hotel room when I was a naïve college grad answering an ad for a job. This was in Chicago, where I had landed on my way to New York to become an actor. Chicago had a theater scene, too, and I thought I'd give it a shot, but after my scary job interview I thought New York is probably safer. Ha!

Supposedly, Mr. Lincoln said, "Think of strangers as friends you haven't met yet." I hate to disagree with Honest Abe, but I rather think of friends as strangers who have proven themselves trustworthy.

Sometimes you yourself feel like a stranger. The song "Stranger in Paradise" is from a Broadway musical called *Kismet*, and became a big hit for Tony Bennett. It tells about the mad love a man has for a beautiful maiden, and when he thinks about her he is in Paradise, a place he's not been before, until he met her, and he calls her an angel and asks her to take his hand, not send him away in dark despair, but open her arms and tell him he is a stranger no more.

My wife is like that.

Paradise is a name for pure love, as in Omar Kayaam's famous line about having a loaf of bread, a jug of wine, "and thou beside me singing in the Wilderness...." The bread, the wine, the song turns the Wilderness into Paradise, so the wine is not Two-Buck Chuck from Trader Joe's, that's for certain, but a fine red with a nice nose and bold finish.

And speaking of a nice nose and a bold finish, I can't help thinking of Charlton Heston in *Ben-Hur*. Classic profile, and the chariot race at the end is one of the great action sequences ever filmed, way before CG, using real horses and stuntmen, one of whom died in the filming of it.

I always liked Heston, a decent man, excellent actor, married to the same woman for 64 years--a rarity in Hollywood. I remember going to the movies with my mom and dad to see *Planet of the Apes,* and when Heston finally recovers his voice and says, "Get your stinkin' paws off me, you damn dirty ape!" my mom laughed and clapped with delight. I loved it when my mom laughed.

"I believe our Heavenly Father invented man because he was disappointed in the monkey. I believe that whenever a human being, of even the highest intelligence and culture, delivers an opinion upon a matter apart from his particular and especial line of interest, training and experience, it will always be an opinion of so foolish and so valueless a sort that it can be depended upon to suggest our Heavenly Father that the human being is another disappointment and that he is no considerable improvement upon the monkey." – Mark Twain

I heard of a pastor who was offering a series of children's sermons on the symbols of the church. One Sunday the pastor talked to the kids about vestments and asked the question, "Why do you think I wear this collar?" A little boy raised his hand. "Because it kills ticks and fleas for up to five months?"

SIGNS—I MEAN BILLBOARDS—OF THE TIMES

Jerome Bengis died, in Florida. He was the owner of the family business, Bengis Signs, a billboard company his father, Moe Bengis, built.

Indeed, Moe Bengis designed one of the most famous billboards of all time, for Coppertone. It showed a little blond-haired girl in a swimsuit, with a cocker spaniel pulling down the bottoms with its teeth. The sign was motorized, so the bathing suit went down and up, alternately exposing and covering the little girl's behind. Why? To reveal a definite tan line.

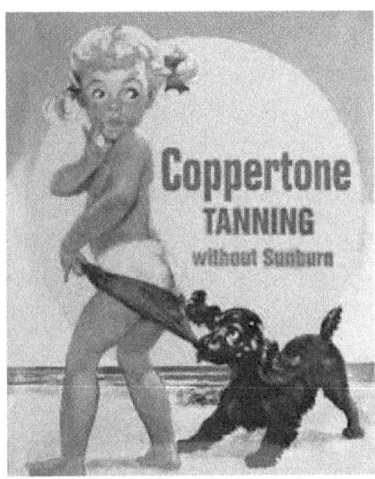

When Coppertone started out, it produced suntan lotion, not sunscreen, meaning it purportedly helped you deepen your tan...like copper, you see?

On radio and TV the commercials sang, "Tan, don't burn. Get a Coppertone tan."

Hundreds of these billboards went up along the east coast. But there was one I remember in SoCal because it was along the 5 freeway on the way to Disneyland. I looked for it as a kid, knowing it meant we were almost to Walt's place.

Over time, the mechanical signs became too expensive to operate. But the original still stands on Biscayne Boulevard in Miami, the monthly upkeep and insurance paid for by Merck, now the parent company of Coppertone.

> *I think that I shall never see*
> *A billboard lovely as a tree.*
> *Indeed, unless the billboards fall*
> *I'll never see a tree at all.*
> –Ogden Nash

A plucky approach to roadside signage appeared during the Great Depression, by a plucky family business hustling a "brushless shaving cream" called Burma-Shave. Things weren't going so well. The boss of the outfit, Clinton M. Odell, was looking for ad ideas when his son Allan suggested a new concept—a series of six signs with one line on them adding up to an amusing snapper at the end. The signs would be one hundred feet apart along the road, giving drivers a few seconds to read each one as they anticipated the next.

Nobody liked the idea…until the signs started to appear.

DOES YOUR HUSBAND
MISBEHAVE
GRUNT AND GRUMBLE
RANT AND RAVE
SHOOT THE BRUTE SOME
BURMA-SHAVE

DON'T STICK
YOUR ELBOW
OUT SO FAR
IT MAY GO HOME
IN ANOTHER CAR
BURMA SHAVE

The Burma-Shave signs were a hit and sales took off. Because something else took off at the same time, America's love of the car—like the affordable Model T Ford. And during the Depression, the signs were light entertainment amidst the gloom. "They were pleasant," Allan's son recalls. "Back in 1929, '30, '31, things were tougher in this country, and people enjoyed them because they were happy. They weren't anything that was discouraging or upsetting."

Exactly the philosophy of Whimsical Wanderings.

Another famous sign also featured a blonde. Her name was—and still is—Angelyne. Billboards of this zaftig lass, wearing shades over pouty lips, were splashed across Los Angeles in the 1980s, leading us Angelenos to ask: Who is Angelyne? What is she famous for?

The answer eventually came: she was famous for making herself famous.

Her real name is Ronia Goldberg and she had designs on becoming a singing sensation. A wealthy businessman met her and started the billboard campaign, which eventually reached nearly 200 signs in and around L.A.

Angelyne here, Angelyne there. You couldn't get away from her and her pink Corvette. She was the California version of Dr. T. J. Eckleburg. Her eyes were always upon you.

Singing stardom didn't come to Angelyne, but that didn't

stop her from becoming a fixture in popular culture, with spot scenes in movies and TV shows. Not to mention live sightings in her Corvette tooling around the Sunset Strip and Hollywood.

She even ran for Governor of California. Twice.

The first time was after the administrations of Jerry Brown and Gray Davis, resulting in her political catchphrase: *We've had Brown and Gray. Now how about some blonde and pink?*

She got 2,536 votes.

Marcus Aurelius, the Stoic philosopher who also ran Rome for awhile, said, "After fame, oblivion." Andy Warhol, not a Stoic philosopher but a pop artist, famously prognosticated that in the future everyone would be world famous for at least 15 minutes.

So, if you average things out, most people will get famous then go back to oblivion after 16 minutes or so.

Which is why people try so hard to "go viral" on social media. (Don't you wish some of them would go bacterial?)

The craziest, wildest, weirdest, angriest posts get the most "clicks." No more room for reasoned, nuanced thought pieces. No more hour-long conversations between well-behaved rivals, like on the old *Firing Line* TV show. William F. Buckley, Jr. and his guests—usually of differing political philosophies—would discuss actual ideas that made people actually think. Oh, the humanity!

Buckley, of course, was known for his Ivy League accent and penchant for using ten-dollar words where a buck-and-a-half word would suffice.

Which means that Buckley wouldn't get much attention today, unless he started crying and shouting, "LEAVE BRITNEY ALONE! YOU CAN'T EXPECT HER TO DECOT MATTERS OF THE FIRST PHILOSOPH-

ICAL MAGNITUDE FROM AND EXAMINATION OF HER OWN ORDURE!"

Think about that!

"When the sun goes below the horizon it is not set; the heavens glow for a full hour after its departure. And when a great and good man sets, the sky of this world is luminous long after he is out of sight. Such a man cannot die out of this world. When he goes he leaves behind him much of himself. Being dead, he speaks." – Henry Ward Beecher

"The most costly of all follies is to believe passionately in the palpably not true. It is the chief occupation of mankind." – H. L. Mencken

SPIDERS, MYTHS, AND BURT LANCASTER'S TEETH

Random noun: *Spiderling*.

I was not familiar with this word. It means "young spider." They have spider age differentials? Is there a "spiderteen"? Do mothers warn their spiderlings not to wander off because there's a monster out there holding a giant broom?

Fear of spiders is *arachnophobia*. It's called that because of an ancient myth about a woman named Arachne. (I don't know what baby name scroll was popular in those days, but they sure could have used another one.) According to the Roman poet Ovid, Arachne was a weaver of surpassing skill, and wasn't shy about saying so. She boasted she could out-weave Minerva herself.

Minerva was a goddess who had several domains to look after, like poetry, medicine, website design, and weaving. "Who does this little strumpet think she is?" Minerva said to

herself one day. (Editorial note: This is drawn from the

JSB translation of the Ovid poem, based on a complete inability to read Latin.)

Minerva disguised herself as an old crone (which is the only kind of crone there is; their young are called *cronelings*) and warned Arachne that insulting the gods was not a good career move. But if she were to confess her sin, Minerva was prepared to forgive her.

Arachne scoffed at this, and said if Minerva thought she was so great she ought to come down and have a weaving contest. Minerva whipped off her old crone outfit and said, "Game on, sweetie!" [JSB trans.]

They immediately sat at their looms and started weaving tapestries. Minerva chose to depict scenes of gods punishing mortals for various sins, like pride, hubris, and letting man buns become a fashion.

Arachne's tapestry was like a tabloid TV show. It depicted Zeus deflowering various maidens, as he was wont to do. And it was one beautiful piece of art.

Minerva had to admit as much, but she was enraged about this insult to the king of the gods. Not being a good sport, Minerva took her shuttle—a wooden tool used on a loom—and slammed it over Arachne's dome, and then destroyed the tapestry.

This was too much shaming for Arachne. She hanged herself. When Minerva found out, she felt some pity for the girl (from which we get the Latin phrase *Tibi gratias ago pro nihilo*—"Thanks for nothing.")

And how did Minerva demonstrate her compassion? She turned Arachne into a spider (the Romans had odd ideas about compassion in those days).

In this way, the spawn of Arachne would go on weaving forever. And it's a pretty incredible thing that spiders do, when you realize they can put up a web overnight and the thing is as beautiful and symmetrical as Burt Lancaster's teeth.

Lancaster is one of my favorite actors. He started out as a circus acrobat, which is why he did most of his own stunts in the movies. See *The Crimson Pirate* sometime. He was 39 when he did that, and he was flipping and trapezing like a man half his age. That was in 1952.

In 1966 he made a great film called *The Professionals*. He was 53 then and climbed up a sheer rock face, ascending with a fixed rope. Think Brad Pitt could do *that*?

Lancaster had what can't be taught or bought—charisma. The camera loved him. He dominates every scene he's in. Among my favorite Lancaster movies:

The Killers
From Here to Eternity
Criss Cross
Elmer Gantry
The Professionals
Valdez is Coming
Seven Days in May

That last one was written by the great Rod Serling, and co-starred Lancaster's friend Kirk Douglas. Burt plays a four-star general, a military hero and chairman of the Joint Chiefs of Staff. Kirk is his assistant. Kirk begins to suspect that Burt is planning a military coup. The movie is taut and suspenseful all the way through, and has one of the best closing lines ever.

Spoiler Alert

By the end, the coup has been squelched. Burt is through. As he's walking out of the Pentagon, Kirk is coming in. Kirk, without any pleasure, hands him an official letter.

Burt: Are you sufficiently up on your Bible to know who Judas was?
Kirk: I suggest you read that letter, sir. It's from the president.
Burt: I asked you a question.
Kirk: Are you ordering me to answer, sir?
Burt: I am!
Kirk: Yes, I know who Judas was. He was a man I worked for and admired, until he disgraced the four stars on his uniform.

Boom! For a writer, there's nothing quite as satisfying as great last line. I work on mine more than any other part of a novel. Rumor has it that in the first draft of *Gone With the Wind,* the last line was: "Tomorrow will probably suck, too." Good thing Margaret Mitchell thought it through.

Some of my favorite last lines:

He turned out the light and went into Jem's room. He would be there all night, and he would be there when Jem waked up in the morning. (*To Kill a Mockingbird* by Harper Lee)

The creatures outside looked from pig to man, and from man to pig, and from pig to man again; but already it was impossible to say which was which. (*Animal Farm* by George Orwell)

It's funny. Don't ever tell anybody anything. If you do, you start missing everybody. (*The Catcher in the Rye* by J. D. Salinger)

I leaned forward and raised her tiny fists and held them against my closed eyes. In that moment I knew all the mysteries were solved. That I was home. That I was saved. (*Lost Light* by Michael Connelly)

I never saw any of them again — except the cops. No way has yet been invented to say goodbye to them. (*The Long Goodbye* by Raymond Chandler)

But for them it was only the beginning of the real story. All their life in this world and all their adventures in Narnia had only been the cover and the title page: now at last they were beginning Chapter One of the Great Story which no one on earth has read: which goes on forever: in which every chapter is better than the one before. (*The Last Battle* by C. S. Lewis)

And what I am writing here is the last line of this Whimsical Wandering.

TAKE ME OUT TO THE OLD BALLGAME WITH THE ANDREWS SISTERS

Random word: *Ballpark.*

We talk about ballpark figures, as in, "Give me a ballpark." It's an estimate of a number so a preliminary decision can be made, subject to later revision. The term comes from the old radio days of baseball, when the announcer would look at the crowd in the ballpark and estimate how many people were in attendance.

That used to be a wonderful concept, a park wherein men played a game, and you could spend a few hours (or more, depending on whether the game went to extra innings) relaxing in a seat with a bag of peanuts and a hot dog. No stress, no strain, unless you got exercised at an umpire's call. Total cost in the old days, a few bucks to twenty, depending on where your seat was and how much you ate.

Now to take a family of four to a game involves a second mortgage (and that's just a ballpark figure).

My first sight of a real ballpark was when I was eight and

my dad took me to Dodger Stadium. We walked up some stairs then into the stadium. Everything was dull and gray and in the shadows, and then I saw it for the first time, the field! The grass, so green and lush, and the infield, reddish brown like a caramel blanket.

We sat and watched the teams get ready, the Dodgers in blue and white and the Pittsburgh Pirates in black and yellow, and my dad made a motion with his hand to a peanut vendor who threw him a bag, then my dad passed money to the guy next him and so on to the end of the row.

Then the biggest man in the world, dressed in a Dodger uniform, came out to the pitcher's mound and started throwing the ball to the catcher, and the ball went so fast, faster than I'd ever seen. His name was Don Drysdale.

A few years later my dad and mom and I went to visit the home of my dad's friend John, who lived in a gated community called Hidden Hills, with big lots and even horses, and John's son, Craig, who was my age, told me Don Drysdale was their next-door neighbor, and would I like to meet him? I said, "Would I ever!" So he took me to the house, which had the biggest front door in the world, and he knocked, and the door opened and there he was, filling the entire doorway, Don Drysdale, and Craig said this is my friend Jim, and Big D stuck out his hand and I shook it, and my hand disappeared completely. Then he took a postcard sized photo of himself in uniform and autographed it for me. I still have it in a scrapbook, right next to my postcard sized autographed photo of Sandy Koufax.

For me, there's no ballpark figure here. They are priceless.

Ballparks used to be in every town in the old days, though the old days were not all good days, especially for the African American ballplayers who were shut out of major league baseball for so many years, until Jackie Robinson broke the color barrier (my dad was the catcher on the UCLA baseball team, and a teammate of Robinson's. I treasure the team photo that hangs on my office wall).

The black players were consigned to what they called the Negro Leagues, and so many great ones will never be remembered.

Two who will be are Satchel Paige and James Bell. That's right, James "Cool Papa" Bell. He was reputed to be the fastest man in all of baseball, and was Paige's roomie. A reporter once asked Paige how fast Cool Papa Bell really was. Satch said, "He's so fast he can turn off the lights and be in bed before the room gets dark."

Random noun: *Oldie.*

An oldie but a goody, they used to say, a semi-apologetic way of introducing a song or a joke or a show from the past, when usually no apology is necessary, for the newies are not often goodies these days.

Old songs. Has anyone improved on the sound of the Andrews Sisters? No, though the Pippini Sisters come close to being equal. But Patti, LaVerne and Maxene could boogie-woogie harmony like wild angels stepping out of the heavenly chorus.

"Boogie-Woogie Bugle Boy" was their most famous song, and you can see them perform it in the Abbott and Costello movie Buck Privates. You just can't be sad listening to the Andrews Sisters, as opposed to the angst-ridden or expletive-laced noise now shattering the airwaves.

Old movies are far and away goodier than most of the screen stains we are subject to now. Put me on a desert island with a small theater that serves popcorn, and I'd choose Double Indemnity, Citizen Kane, Casablanca, Shane, The Best Years of Our Lives, High Noon, Some Like It Hot, Lover Come Back, Spartacus, All About Eve, Stalag 17, Out of the Past, Sergeant York, The Awful Truth, His Girl Friday, Lawrence of Arabia, Singin' in the Rain, Rear Window, Sunset Blvd., On the Waterfront, It's a Wonderful Life, Shadow of a Doubt, To Kill a Mockingbird, The Maltese Falcon, It Happened One Night, North by Northwest, Duck Soup, Horsefeathers, Hail the Conquering Hero, Modern Times, 12 Angry Men, Swing Time, Ben-Hur...and each showing preceded by a Warner Bros. cartoon featuring Bugs Bunny and/or Daffy Duck.

Not to say that all things new are bad. Just in general (which reminds me to put Buster Keaton's The General on the list).

"Be who you is, 'cause if you ain't who you is, you is who you ain't." – Brennan Manning

FERTILIZER DISCIPLINE

Pearl Berg died at the age of 114. She was designated the ninth oldest person in the world by the Gerontology Research Group, which must have Sherpa guides in the Himalayas scoping out old people and asking them when they were born.

Pearl was born in 1909, which was a good year for births. Benny Goodman was born that year. So was Errol Flynn. Also Frances Dee, who was a beautiful actress in the early days of Hollywood. She was married to Joel McCrea and stayed married to him from 1933 until his death in 1990, which makes it as rare in Hollywood marriages as the Blue-Footed Booby in the Galapagos.

Dee herself made it to age 94.

Joel McCrea was one of the most decent men ever to achieve movie stardom, not letting celebrity go to his head, and holding to a strong set of values, as my own father found out one day. You see, my grandfather built a house on Nichols Canyon Road in Hollywood in 1923, and later Joel

McCrea moved in next door where there was land for him to keep horses.

When my father was a lad he was chatting with Joel McCrea in one of the stalls. Dad uttered a very bad word, not apt for one so young as he. In response, Joel McCrea did what a father used to do in those days, which was wash out a boy's mouth with soap, only there wasn't any soap around, so Joel McCrea used a bit of fertilizer.

Don't be shocked. Such was the way men in those days. They looked out for the boys in the neighborhood, helped keep them of trouble, but on occasion when the father of the child was not around (as my grandfather was not, being on the road as a traveling salesman for Encyclopedia Britannica) a man might step in *in loco parentis* and do some disciplining. My father remembered Joel McCrea with great affection and admiration.

McCrea is known today primarily for four films: *Foreign Correspondent, Sullivan's Travels, The Palm Beach Story* and *Ride the High Country*. But his favorite film of his, and a hidden gem, is *Stars in My Crown*. The script was written by a woman named Margaret Fitts, about whom very little was known. There was no biographical entry for her on IMDB, only a few movie and TV credits, and then, whoosh, by 1962 she was gone from the business.

With my film professor son doing research at the Academy of Motion Pictures Arts and Sciences, we managed to find a phone number down San Diego way. I called it. A woman answered. It was, indeed, Margaret Fitts. She was 86, two years before her death. Sharp as a tack, she allowed me to interview her. My son did up a little bio for her and posted it at IMDB:

Margaret Fitts grew up in Los Angeles. She graduated from Stanford University in 1945, where she studied speech, drama and journalism. She wrote a regular column for the Stanford Daily in her senior year. Ms. Fitts applied to the junior writers' program at MGM and was accepted, signing a studio contract in 1947. Her scripts were primarily adaptations, a noted exception being her original story and screenplay, *The King and Four Queens*. After leaving MGM in 1954 she worked in television for a time, then retired from the film business.

I'm happy that is up there, preserved for those lucky ones in the future who discover *Stars in My Crown*.

I had my own mouth washed out with soap once that I recall. It was my mother who did the cleaning after I'd defied her with a word that I'd heard adults say after a few beers, and I can still see her face, shock all over it as she hauled me into the bathroom, grabbed the soap out of the dish and shoved it in my mouth. To this day I watch my doggone words with care.

And so should we all.

"Words have a longer life than deeds." – Pindar (518 BC – 438 BC)

THE DAY I MET THE ALL-AMERICAN GIRL

Sometime back in the late 90s, I went to a local Kinko's to make some copies. As I waited, an elegant older lady next to me rolled out a large photo on the counter. It was a gorgeous picture of three lovely young ladies. From the hairstyles, I guessed it was early 1940s.

I couldn't help myself. "Beautiful!"

"My sisters and me," the lady said.

"You look like movie stars."

"We made some pictures."

This turned out to be the understatement of the year.

"Really?" I said. "What were some of the titles?"

"Have you seen Sergeant York or Yankee Doodle Dandy?"

"Oh, man, I love those..." I looked at the photo and back at her. "Wait a second. Joan Leslie!"

Joan Leslie, center, with her sisters

She smiled. I think she was floored that I, way up here in the 1990s, knew who she was. How could I not? Any fan of those movies knows Joan Leslie. In the 1940s she was the All-American Girl, the Girl Next Door, the wife of Jimmy Cagney in *Dandy* and the intended of Gary Cooper in *York*.

She was a special favorite of the GIs in WWII. In fact, in the movie *Hollywood Canteen* (1944)—which featured several big stars of the day—Joan Leslie was the plot focus: the millionth GI to visit the Canteen got to go on a date with her.

Needless to say, her star was rising.

Until after the war.

Joan Leslie was born in 1925. During the Depression her father lost his job, so she and her sisters performed a musical act in vaudeville to put food on the table.

CINNAMON BUNS AND MILK BONE UNDERWEAR

Sister act to the accompaniment of their mother's accordion was a favorite pastime when the Brodell family first came to Hollywood two years ago on the strength of Joan's contract with M-G-M. Mary, 24 (*left*), is now married and living in Washington with her husband who is studying navigation. Betty, 21 (*right*), hopes to go in to radio work, buses daily to her singing lessons, still lives with the family. LIFE Photographer Bob Landry took these pictures of Joan when she was a very young starlet, her career all before her.

Life Magazine profile, Oct. 26, 1942

They were spotted by an MGM talent scout and Joan, age 11, got a studio contract paying $200 a week. But she was let go six months later because the studio decided to concentrate on another young performer by the name of Frances Gumm. (Never heard of Frances Gumm? You might know her by her movie name: Judy Garland.)

Joan went on to do some freelance work for other studios. Then, in 1941, she was signed by Warner Bros. At the tender age of 16 she got the part in *Sergeant York*. The movie was a hit. Then came *Yankee Doodle Dandy*, and Joan Leslie was a star.

Joan Leslie and Gary Cooper in Sergeant York

She was also a staunch Catholic. After the war, films got grittier and women's roles more suggestive. Joan didn't like the scripts she was being offered, objected to the immorality in some, and requested she be released from her contract. Jack Warner, the martinet mogul, refused.

So she took him to court. And won.

As a result, the villain Warner made sure she was blackballed by the other big studios. Joan would make a few more movies for "Poverty Row" but never again a major motion picture. In the 1960s she moved into television guest spots and kept that up until her retirement in 1991.

Joan Leslie died in 2015 at the age of 90, with her faith and integrity held high.

Which is more than I can say for Jack Warner.

I love it that I got to meet, completely by chance, one of the stars of the golden age of Hollywood. Also a personal favorite because of her roles in two of my all-time fave movies. Next time you watch *Sergeant York* or *Yankee Doodle Dandy*, you'll have an added appreciation because of the presence of the beautiful, wonderful All-American Girl—Joan Leslie.

DRIVING A FIRE HAZARD TO THE PROM

Random word: *Interject*.

To put something in, usually during a conversation when someone else is speaking, e.g., "If I may interject?"

One of the most famous interjections happened during Napoleon's fateful march toward Moscow, when he was telling his generals to quit complaining about the cold (he was wrapped in a bear-skin blanket when he said this, by the way, and would wear that same blanket when he got his frozen behind out of Russia, leaving his men behind), and one of his men, the cook in fact, said, "May I interject, *mon* general?" to which Napoleon said, "No! Now make me a flaky pastry that I can name after myself."

History would have taken a different tack had the French conqueror listened to his advisers who wanted to interject, "You want to march on Moscow? Have you ever been to Russia in the winter?"

I wonder if other historical persons made, or failed to

make decisions based upon interjections or lack thereof? Such as, "General Custer, there's a whole boatload of Indians over that ridge and I don't think we have the manpower to take them on alone."

Or, "Captain, I think we'd better be on the lookout for icebergs, and by the way, there's a kid on board making a nuisance of himself drawing scandalous pictures of women in automobiles."

Speaking of which, the first automobile I owned was a hand-me-down Ford Pinto from my dad, and that's what I drove my date in to the high school prom, and luckily was not rear-ended as the Pinto was a notorious fireball waiting to happen.

So there I was, all dressed up, and my girlfriend all dressed up, and along came a car with some guys in it, the kind without prom dates, and they thought they'd have some sport with us by driving on our right on the two lanes of Ventura Boulevard in such a way as to deny me the ability to turn into the school parking lot. I would slow, and they would slow, and I knew the game, so I rammed the gas pedal which shot that Pinto up to 30 mph at least, as the other car sped up, too, but I had a plan.

I timed things perfectly, and told my girl to get ready, then hit the brakes...the other car sped on past, and I quickly turned right onto a side street that led to the back of the high school, and took us around the block and into the parking lot, and that I believe was the only known instance of a dynamic maneuver by a Ford Pinto in automotive history, to which I add this interjection: "I may be right." To which I further add, in the immortal words of Billy Joel, "I may be crazy, but it just may be a lunatic you're looking for."

Lee Iacocca, by the way, was the Ford executive behind the hugely popular Mustang. He thought Ford needed a subcompact car to compete with Volkswagen and Japanese imports, so got behind the Pinto (fortunately, he didn't rear-end one) and they rushed production. They became aware of a fuel tank problem (like, the possibility of a fiery explosion!) and thought of some solutions, like lining the fuel tank with a nylon bladder, or putting a plastic baffle between the fuel tank and the differential housing. Each of these would add a few bucks to the cost of producing a car, so they didn't do them. The following year a Pinto got rear ended, became a fireball, and killed the driver and burned a young passenger, resulting in a lawsuit that ended up costing Ford around $5 million, not including lawyer fees.

The most infamous fire in history may be the one Mrs. O'Leary's cow caused in Chicago in 1871. They even wrote a song about it.

> Late one night, when we were all in bed,
> Mrs. O'Leary lit a lantern in the shed.
> Her cow kicked it over,
> Then winked her eye and said,
> "There'll be a hot time in the old town tonight!"

My son made up a joke when he was four. "What did the fire say to the house?...I'm terrifrying!" Not bad for four.

"An ounce of prevention is worth a pound of cure." – Benjamin Franklin, 1736, to the city fathers of Philadelphia warning them about fire hazards

"Adam and Eve were the first of all unions to defy management." – Evan Esar

GROWING WINGS ON THE WAY DOWN

Random word: *wing*.

You can take someone under your wing. You can also take the person under your wing to a wingding, which is a "lively, wild or lavish party" (as opposed to dingbat fonts developed by Microsoft, which are cute but not lively).

It's good to "take wing," to leave the nest, to fly. As a writer, I like to take wing. Ray Bradbury used to say, "Jump off a cliff and grow wings on the way down." He meant that writers should let their imaginations leap into the unknown, where the subconscious dreams, write it all down and only later figure out what it all means.

Sort of like marriage.

In the 1920s there was a fad called "wing walking," where a daredevil would go aloft in a biplane, then step out on one of the wings and wave to the movie camera in another plane, or at the crowd on the ground that *oohed* and *ahhed*.

A man named Ormer Locklear is credited with originating the stunt in 1918. He developed another trick where he actually changed planes in mid air. Without a parachute.

Then the ladies got into the act. A young woman named Ethel Johnson, 17, who was working as a trapeze artist with the Barnum and Bailey Circus, answered an ad looking for a woman daredevil. She got the job (and a new name: Ethel Dare) and became the first woman to do the change planes trick.

Sadly, in 1924 she fell to her death.

But another wing-walking woman, Gladys Ingle, performed into the 1930s and lived to the age of 82. Her most famous stunt was going up in a plane with a spare wheel tethered to her back, then climbing onto a plane that was missing a wheel, and replacing it right there in the clouds. You can see it on YouTube. I've watched it, and it gives me the heebie jeebies. I'm not great with heights to begin with.

She's never missed yet. Miss Gladys Ingle, famous stunt girl of the air, standing on the upper wing of a plane 5,000 feet above the ground, ready to swing onto the second plane. The pilot of the upper plane (shown in the second cockpit), is Art Goebel, transcontinental flight champion. Miss Ingle is the only girl dare-devil

The term "heebie jeebies" was coined by a cartoonist

named Billy DeBeck, in 1923, in his cartoon strip "Barney Google."

But the term really took off when the great Louis Armstrong recorded a song called "Heebie Jeebies" in 1926.

Keith Sperry died in Fairborn, OH, at the age of 73. His obit is short, just a notice of where his "celebration of life" will be held, and how someone can "plant trees in his memory."

Which reminded me of a line from the old radio comedian Fred Allen, who had an ongoing "feud" with Jack Benny. (It was all in good fun, and also good for ratings). In 1939, Benny's hometown of Waukegan, Illinois, planted an elm tree in front of City Hall as a tribute to the star. Some months later, however, the tree died.

This prompted Allen to quip on his show: "How can a tree live in Waukegan when the sap is in California?"

The word *sap*, meaning someone who is a taco short of a combination plate, comes from an old English insult, *sapskull*, a skull filled with the soft, sticky stuff inside a tree.

When hardboiled detective fiction took off in the 1920s, *sap* had two meanings: a) sucker, stooge, fool; and b) a leather pouch about a foot long filled with lead, used to whap someone on the head (also known as a *blackjack*).

We all feel like saps sometimes, and also feel like we've been whapped over the head by events, trials, tribulations, politics, social media, accidents, injuries, deaths, Kardashians, tsunamis, fires, earthquakes, egg prices, and Daylight Savings Time.

When that happens we can stew, or doom scroll, or snap at a loved one. Or eat ice cream out of the tub. Or go to Tommy's for a chili cheese dog and fries (though I will admit this is one of my guilty pleasures anyway, Tommy's being an L.A. institution since 1946, and any eatery that lasts that long in our fair city deserves to be frequented, just like Musso & Frank on Hollywood Boulevard, feeding movie stars and writers since 1919, and where you can sit in the booth favored by Charlie Chaplin, or Raymond Chandler's favorite).

So to keep from being sapped by life you've got to do something that is balm to the soul, not just *think* about doing something. Like play with your grandboys who are still at the age where sticks are swords and garbage can lids are shields.

If you write, as I do, you write your way out. Another Bradbury quote: "You must stay drunk on writing so reality cannot destroy you."

I met Ray Bradbury once, when he spoke at a branch of the L.A. library, the branch I grew up in, in Woodland Hills. This was back when I was an unpublished writer unsure if I had the goods. I was reading books on writing, and one I treasured was Bradbury's *Zen in the Art of Writing*.

I took my well-thumbed and underlined copy of *Zen* to the library and settled in with a packed room. Bradbury arrived, walking slowly and wearing his white hair long and a bit wild. His hair was a metaphor for his writing approach—let it go, untamed, and put off a neat cut for as long as possible. "Time enough to think and cut and rewrite tomorrow," Bradbury wrote in Zen. "But today—explode—fly apart —disintegrate!"

Bradbury spoke about his love of libraries, and it was great to hear from his own lips the well-known tale of how he wrote *Fahrenheit 451* on a rented typewriter in the basement of UCLA's Powell Library.

He signed books after his talk, so I stood in line with my copy of *Zen*. I introduced myself and we shook hands.

"Are you a writer?" he asked.

I quoted that line from the book: "'Stay drunk on writing so reality cannot destroy you.'"

He laughed and said, "Oh, you must!"

I asked him if he set himself a daily quota. He said, "I let my love determine how much I write."

"Ah, so you fall in love daily?"

"That's right."

He signed my book.

"Do you write every day?" he asked.

"Five days a week," I said. "Weekends are for my family."

He laughed again. "That's the way to do it!" (That's because Bradbury did it this way, too.)

He offered his hand once more and said, "God bless you."

And off I went into the night, feeling blessed indeed for having had the chance to chat with one of the legends of our literature—Ray Bradbury, American original.

"There's nothing to writing. All you do is sit down at a typewriter and open a vein." – Red Smith

CHEST HAIR, HOT DOGS, AND WIENIE WHISTLES

Random word: *Electrocardiogram.*

The ol' EKG, which is where a nurse puts stickers on your chest and attaches wires so they can see what your heart is doing. It's painless, unless you have chest hair, because you have to rip those stickers off when the test is over. It's not death by a thousand cuts, but it's not a warm eucalyptus oil rub, either.

Best to just grip it and rip it.

For a time, chest hair was a fashion statement for men. Hemingway got it started, running away from the bulls in Pamplona, deep sea fishing off the Florida Keys, hunting game in Africa. He wrote a famous story called "Big Two-Hearted River." The original title "Big Hairy-Chested Writer" was thought to be a tad narcissistic.

Sean Connery as James Bond took the hairy chest wide. It influenced me as a junior high student. I told girls my name was Bell...James Bell. This got me nowhere.

Burt Reynolds took the fuzzy torso to new heights—or lows, depending on your perspective—when he became the first nude male centerfold in Cosmopolitan magazine (though he tastefully, and thankfully, placed his hand strategically, so we wouldn't be subjected to his totality).

Burt was always a bit goofy, liked to have fun. He was actually a fine actor, but preferred being in cartoonish fare like *Smokey and the Bandit*.

Indeed, Burt was the first choice to play the astronaut neighbor in *Terms of Endearment*, but he turned it down in order to do a forgettable comedy called *Stroker Ace*.

Thus, Jack Nicholson got the part and ended up with an Academy Award for Best Supporting Actor.

Oops. Burt said that was his biggest regret as an actor.

Speaking of alternative choices, do you know who was originally considered for the part of Mrs. Robinson in *The Graduate*? The part that Ann Bancroft got an Oscar nomination for?

Doris Day.

Don't spit out your coffee. Doris Day would have been perfect for that role. She was the right age, 45 (Bancroft was 36, playing older). She had the right look: the "perfect 50s housewife" who had become an alcoholic while trapped in a loveless marriage.

Also, Doris Day was one of the most talented stars ever to grace the screen. She could sing, dance, and do both drama and comedy. She was at her best as a comedienne, especially in the two classics *Pillow Talk* and *Lover Come Back* (both with her pal Rock Hudson, supported by the hilarious Tony Randall).

Day thought about taking the role, but turned down the part because she felt it would be too much of a shock to her fans.

That's probably true, but I have no hesitation to say she would have knocked that role out of the park and walked off with the Academy Award. (Katharine Hepburn won the Oscar that year for *Guess Who's Coming to Dinner*. A fine performance, but Bancroft should have won.)

The most competitive Best Actress year was 1950. You had two all-time iconic performances—Bette Davis in *All About Eve* and Gloria Swanson in *Sunset Boulevard*. In an upset, Judy Holliday won for the light comedy *Born Yesterday*.

By the way, no one is quite sure how the Academy Award came to be called "Oscar." Some think an Academy librarian remarked that the statuette resembled her Uncle Oscar. There was a story that Bette Davis named it after her first husband, Harmon Oscar Nelson, because she thought the award's rear end resembled her hubby's caboose (Davis let the story be told for a while, then recanted).

But when I think of Oscar, I think of Oscar Mayer wieners.

When I was in elementary school, the Wienermobile came to visit. This was a huge vehicle shaped like an Oscar Mayer wiener, with the logo and everything. It was driven by "Little Oscar," a small man named George Molchan. He gave out "wienie whistles" to the kids. These were also shaped like an Oscar Mayer wiener, and you could toot out the four notes of the Oscar Mayer wiener jingle with it. Or drive your parents crazy. Your choice.

In the Tim Allen movie *The Santa Clause*, the character played by Judge Reinhold talks sadly about the Christmas he'd wished for a wienie whistle that never came. At the end of the movie, the new Santa (Allen) drops him one, making a Christmas believer out of him.

That's hot dog power.

When I lived in New York I frequented Nathan's, the best dog joint ever, slathering on mustard and topping it off with sauerkraut.

But I was never tempted to enter the Nathan's hot dog eating contest held every July 4th at Coney Island.

Are you kidding me? Shoveling as many dogs down your gullet as you can in ten minutes? A guy named Joey Chestnut dominated the contest for many years, setting the record of seventy (70!) downed dogs.

But that's not all. He set records for eating pulled pork sandwiches, Philly cheesesteaks, Taco Bell tacos, and a host of other like items.

How is this fellow still alive?

To me, this defeats the whole purpose of the glorious hot dog. A good one is to be savored.

The best was the old Dodger Dog served at Dodger Stadium, back when they were grilled Farmer John all-beef wieners. That was also when you could go to a game without taking out a second mortgage on your home. You put on mustard and topped it with lots of diced onions. Then you took your time munching while watching batting practice. After that, you ate a bag of peanuts as the game unfolded, tossing the shells under your seat.

That was living.

"A hot dog at the ballgame beats roast beef at the Ritz." – Humphrey Bogart

"Nobody, I mean nobody, puts ketchup on a hot dog." – Dirty Harry Callahan

AT LEAST I WAS READY FOR MY NEW YORK MOMENT

Winston Conrad "Wink" Martindale died at the age of 91. He was best known as the genial host of such game shows as "Gambit" and "Tic-Tac-Dough." Indeed, a lot of dough he made, as game show hosts do. The late Alex Trebek of "Jeopardy" fame made an Everest of green, taping shows just three times a week. Another winner of those sweepstakes is the recently retired Pat Sajak of "Wheel of Fortune." Emphasis on fortune. An easy gig, especially compared to digging ditches or practicing law.

I had a chance to hop aboard that gravy train (possibly) when I was fresh out of college. I made some side money performing walk-around magic in bars and restaurants, and the occasional kid's show, once at the famous Magic Castle in Hollywood.

And once for a Boy Scout troop. As I stepped out onto the auditorium stage I looked at the front row and saw a familiar face, that of Mr. Larry Hovis, the comic actor who gained fame in the sitcom *Hogan's Heroes*.

I began my routine with the color-changing silks, and

after the big finish I saw Hovis's expression of smiling awe. I was a hit!

After the show Hovis came up to me. He complimented me on the performance and said he was working with Ralph Edwards Productions. I knew that name. Edwards produced some of the most popular game shows on TV. Hovis gave me his card and said, "Call us and set up an appointment."

Ah, the folly of youth. I was intent on becoming an actor, a serious actor, a Marlon Brando who went to New York to study for the stage, and thence to the movies for immortal stardom.

Game show host? Me? Never would I sink to that level.

Hoo boy.

I never made the call. What would life have been like if I had?

Well, you know how that goes. You've seen *It's a Wonderful Life*. If I'd made the choice, maybe I would have been a multi-millionaire. But then again, I probably wouldn't have met my lovely wife, and that's a price I would never pay.

I did go to New York. And I did act on the stage.

I was freshly arrived in New York City and living at The Leo House on West 23d. Across the street at that time was the Roundabout Theater. I walked over there one day and asked for a job. I got one, pushing around scenery for their current production, Shaw's *You Never Can Tell*.

As part of the deal, I got to audition for their upcoming production of *Othello*.

And I got the part! My first paid acting role! As ... Attendant. No lines, but I didn't care. I was doing Shakespeare Off-Broadway, in tights and everything!

Earle Hyman was Othello. Also in the cast was a young Powers Boothe as Roderigo.

And so we began rehearsals. I loved every minute of it,

even though my part was just walking on, standing, and walking off. But when I was off, I'd listen. I'd listen to how Earle and Nicholas Kepros (Iago) did Shakespeare. Iago has some of the best lines in the entire canon, and I determined to play that role someday.

In fact, one night before the show I was sitting backstage with Earle. He was so generous to the young actors, down-to-earth and always willing to give advice. I mentioned I wanted to play Iago someday, and he said, "You're perfect for it!"

"I am?" I said, wondering if some nefarious part of my personality had leaked out.

"Oh, yes," Earle said. "You have an open, honest face." (This, mind you, was well before I went to law school.) He explained, "Othello calls him 'honest, honest Iago.' It's wrong to play the part as an obvious villain."

I then breezily but sincerely told him I was going to mount a production of *Othello* someday and play Iago, and that I wanted him to play the lead.

"I'll do it!" he said.

A lovely man.

So the show opened and was well received by the *Times*. I continued to listen. I was something of a voice impersonator in those days. I'd crack up the cast by doing imitations of the various actors.

Then one night it happened. My big moment.

Now, to fully appreciate what I'm about to relate it is necessary that you know the classic film *All About Eve*. If you have not seen it and wish to be spared knowing the plot twist, you might want to skip to the last paragraphs of this post.

In brief, *All About Eve* is the story of a theater diva named Margo Channing (Bette Davis). A devoted young fan named Eve Harrington (Anne Baxter) comes to her and pours out her heart about loving the theater and idolizing Margo. This gets her a job as Margo's assistant.

What we come to learn is that Eve Harrington has only one thought in mind—to displace Margo as the star of a new hit play. She underhandedly snags the understudy role. And then she sets in motion an elaborate scheme so Margo will be unable to make curtain one night.

Eve is a sensation, and from there turns her back on everyone who's helped her as she ascends the stairway to stardom.

Back to *Othello*. One night, about an hour and half before curtain, a call comes in from the actor playing Montano—a minor role, but with significant lines. He was stuck in Brooklyn and wouldn't be able to make the show. I can't remember why, but I assure you I had nothing to do with it.

The stage manager was in a panic. There were no understudies. Then someone told him, "Jim knows the part. He knows *all* the parts."

The stage manager rushed over to me and put his hands on my shoulders. "Do you? Do you really know the part?"

"What from the cape can you discern at sea?" I said, quoting Montano's first line.

"You're going on!"

On! Me! I was giddy as he spent twenty minutes with me on the stage, walking me through the blocking. I only half listened, for my other half was loop-quoting the Bard: "Yet heavens have glory for this victory!"

Then I was dismissed to go get ready for the performance.

As I entered the dressing room, everyone was already putting on makeup or getting into costume. The moment I appeared our Iago, Nick Kepros, in a voice dripping with droll amusement and loud enough for all to hear, said, "Well, well, if it isn't Eve Harrington!"

The room exploded in laughter. It was the perfect line, brilliantly delivered.

So on I went.

Nailed it!

Though it was one night only and did not catapult me to stardom, it was supremely satisfying. I had spoken Shakespeare on a stage in New York! And received warm congratulations from the cast, including Mr. Earle Hyman.

All that to say, the old saw about luck being the intersection of preparation and opportunity applies.

So prepare!

"An actor's success has the life expectancy of a small boy about to look into the gas tank with a lighted match." – Fred Allen

PUNNY YOU SHOULD ASK

Freddie Joe Blake died in Bridgeport, Ohio, at the age of 69. That's a year younger than I, and those numbers keep popping up in random obits, and I realize I'm starting to outlive so many who were born in the 1950s, which sets me to pondering things like, well, death. It's always time to check and make sure your papers are in order, and Mr. Blake did, for his obit gives us two items about his life—that he was "a railroad worker by trade, and a Christian by faith." As the Good Book says: *O death, where is thy sting?*

Which reminds me of a line about the American playwright Clifford Odets (pronounced oh-DETTS), who gained prominence in the 1930s for his politically slanted plays. When he answered the call from Hollywood and wrote a movie for Gary Cooper, the reviewer for the *New York Times* found it tepid and headlined his review: ODETS, WHERE IS THY STING?

Now that's punny. And as radio comedian Fred Allen once said, "Hanging is too good for a man who makes puns; he should be drawn and quoted."

A good pun makes you snort. A bad pun makes you groan. A bad pun is one that requires too great a stretch of the imagination to make it work, as in this groaner: What do you say to a Llama that invites you to a picnic? "Alpaca lunch."

You groan, yes, but you probably smile, too, and that's the whole point. It's what made Groucho and Chico Marx famous.

Chico (pronounced CHICK-oh, and whose real name was Leonard) took on the persona of an Italian immigrant, which meant he often mangled the English language. As in this exchange from *Horse Feathers* (1932). Groucho, playing the part of Prof. Quincy Adams Wagstaff, is trying to get into a speakeasy. Chico (Baravelli) is guarding the door. Wagstaff knocks and Baravelli opens the window. (Note: "Calomel" is a mercury chloride mineral that was marketed as a cure for a spate of ills in the early 20th century.)

Baravelli: Who are you?
Wagstaff: I'm fine, thanks, who are you?
Baravelli: I'm fine too, but you can't come in unless you give the password.

Wagstaff: Well, what's the password?
Baravelli: Aw, no. You gotta tell me. Hey, I tell you what I do. I give you three guesses. It's the name of a fish.
Wagstaff: Is it Mary?
Baravelli: Ha-ha. That's-a no fish.
Wagstaff: She isn't? Well, she drinks like one. Let me see: Is it sturgeon?
Baravelli: Hey, you crazy. Sturgeon, he's a doctor who cuts you open when-a you sick. Now I give you one more chance.
Wagstaff: I got it. Haddock.
Baravelli: That's-a funny. I gotta haddock, too.
Wagstaff: What do you take for a haddock?
Baravelli: Well, sometimes I take-a aspirin, sometimes I take-a calomel.
Wagstaff: Say, I'd walk a mile for a calomel.
Baravelli: You mean chocolate calomel. I like that too, but you no guess it. Hey, what's-a matter, you no understand English? You can't come in here unless you say, "Swordfish." Now I'll give you one more guess.
Wagstaff: Hmm, swordfish, swordfish... I think I got it. Is it "swordfish"?
Baravelli: Ha! That's-a it. You guess it.
Wagstaff: Pretty good, eh?

Swordfish, by the way, is a tasty aquatic dish—especially if garlic butter and lemon zest are involved—but I prefer sea bass. So did comedian George Burns.

Burns often met friends, including Groucho, for Friday lunch at the Hillcrest Country Club. He always ordered sea bass. Which triggered Groucho's pun reflex. In the 1930s the popular singer Sophie Tucker had a hit song, "You've Got To See Mamma Every Night (Or You Can't See Mamma At All)." So after Burns said, "Sea bass," Groucho would say, "If you can't sea bass every night, you can't sea bass at all."

Every time.

Finally, Burns had enough. At the next lunch he called the waiter over and whispered, "I'll have sea bass."

And the waiter leaned over and whispered, "If you can't sea bass every night, you can't sea bass at all."

I also like scallops. If Chico were taking my order, he'd say, "Hey, I got a horse that scallops, too."

Chico was so named because he liked "the chicks." Indeed, he was a womanizer and a gambler and predeceased his famous brothers. Outliving him were Groucho, Harpo, Zeppo and... (answer to a trivia question) Gummo, whose real name was Milton, who didn't like show business and instead became a successful talent agent.

And now, because you are a subscriber to Whimsical Wanderings, I will give you the all-time topper trivia question. Use this at any gathering where people think they know a thing or two about movies.

Ask them to name all the Marx brothers. Most will get Groucho, Harpo and Chico. Others will remember Zeppo.

Invariably, there will be one who, with a smile, says, "Aha, you can't fool me. There was also Gummo, who never appeared in the movies."

To which you will say, "You missed one."

You will receive a howl of protest.

But indeed, there was one more Marx brother. This nugget was unearthed by my friend Steve Stoliar, who was Groucho's secretary in the last few years of Groucho's life (and who wrote a memoir of that time called *Raised Eyebrows*). He and author Hector Arce were working on a book about Groucho. Arce arranged for a copy of Groucho's birth certificate to be sent from New York. When Steve looked at it he noticed something odd. The certificate indicated that baby Groucho had three older brothers. But how could that be when he himself was the third born?

Steve and Arce went to Groucho's bedroom, where he was reading a book. They asked Groucho if his parents had any children, other than Chico and Harpo, born before him.

"Yes," Groucho replied casually. "Their first son was Manfred. He died before I was born."

Steve and Arce exchanged startled looks. Arce asked what Manfred died of.

"Old age," Groucho said, and went back to his book. (The actual cause of death was influenza.)

And so it goes. Some die young, some die old, some die in between. So live life to the full and never challenge Death to a pillow fight...unless you are prepared to handle the reaper cushions.

I'd better go now.

If you see an Apple Store getting robbed, does that make you an iWitness?

WILL THE TRUTH SET YOU FREE?

There was a TV news panel the other day, you know, where four or five talking heads jaw about this or that current event. They were discussing some controversial remarks made by a professional athlete, which set off a firestorm of commentary on social media (could we have fewer firestorms and more modest campfires where we sit around telling jokes and roasting hot dogs? How about that for a change?)

They played a clip of the athlete defending the statements, and saying, in part, "I'm just stating my truth."

To which one of the panelists said, "There is no your truth or my truth, there's only the truth…"

He was immediately interrupted by another panelist, who snapped, "That's not true!"

Think about the ironic absurdity of that objection.

It reminded me of a snippet of conversation I heard at a Starbucks once. Two guys were in a friendly debate, the content of which I do not recall. One guy said, "But is that logical?"

The other, with complete conviction, in an effort to hammer home his point, said, "It's so logical it's ridiculous!"

He was not making a joke.

So in the aforementioned panel we have a fellow stating that there is objective truth, to which another panelist says, "That's not true."

Then I must ask, for such a categorical statement, to what standard is she appealing to uphold her statement? For she was not telling him that he had his truth and she had her truth, but that HIS statement was UNTRUE. She thus denied him the very thing she was trying to defend (the idea that we all have "our own truth") while, at the same time, appealing to an objective measurement of truth, the existence of which she had just denied!

That's not logical, but it is ridiculous.

Is there such a thing as the truth? Socrates thought so and went around asking questions to folks to get them to think about it. Apparently he got a lot of young people thinking, and they started to ask embarrassing questions about what the rulers of Athens were doing to louse things up. For "corrupting the youth of Athens" Socrates was sentenced to death.

That's what the search for the truth can bring you if the "rulers" or "authorities" or "experts" don't like to answer questions.

Which reminds me of a transcript from a criminal trial. A lawyer was questioning a woman who witnessed a shooting that took place during a bar fight, and sustained a bullet wound herself.

LAWYER: You were there when the fight broke out?
WOMAN: Yes, I was.
LAWYER: And were you shot in the fracas?

WOMAN: No, I was shot right here in the side.

There isn't much respect for the truth anymore, even in court. They used to make you put one hand on the Bible and swear to tell "the truth, the whole truth, and nothing but the truth, so help you God." That oath may have meant something when people actually believed in God, or at least didn't want to offend Him if He happens to exist.

Now folks just raise their right hand and "swear or affirm" they will tell the truth, and God has nothing to do with it. What incentive is that? What happens if they lie on the stand? No one (virtually) is ever prosecuted for perjury.

Lying is natural to the natural man. Because the truth sometimes hurts, and sometimes people want to hide things. This penchant for lying now pervades every stratum of society. Recall that actor who fabricated a racially motivated attack on himself, which was quickly discovered to be a hoax. What to do in that situation?

When I was a lad, if you got caught in a lie you hung your head in shame and took your medicine. But now liars, caught red tongued, "double down." They repeat the lie with more conviction. If further evidence pops up against them, they "triple down" and so on down the line, even if no one, not even their own mother, believes them anymore.

The belief now is that you can turn a lie into the truth —"your truth"—if you just keep saying it. And the objective in any controversy is not to find the truth, but to "win" even if you must lie to do it.

When I was in law school they taught us that there's a difference between defense lawyers and prosecutors. Defense lawyers are to hold the government to its burden of proof beyond a reasonable doubt, challenging evidence and making sure law enforcement follows the Constitution. They are to "zealously" defend their client, without suborning perjury.

Prosecutors, on the other hand, are sworn to "seek justice." That means if their case is weak they will seriously consider dropping the charges. Not so much anymore. Prosecutors, especially in high-profile cases, can have an "agenda" where winning a case takes precedence over satisfying Lady Justice, the blindfolded goddess holding the scales in one hand and a sword in the other. The scales are held highest. Fair measure is to be the standard before the sword of punishment is raised.

This ideal goes back to all the ancient codes and the roots of English Common Law. As it says in the Magna Carta (1215 A.D.): "To no one will we sell, to no one will we refuse or delay, right or justice."

"A long line of cases," wrote the English judge Lord Hewart in 1924, "shows that it is not merely of some importance but is of fundamental importance that justice should not only be done, but should be manifestly and undoubtedly be seen to be done…. Nothing is to be done which creates even a suspicion that there has been an improper interference with the course of justice."

I leave it to the reader to determine where we are today in upholding this quest.

By the way, if you have a son or daughter who is thinking of going to law school, or is already there, or maybe just graduated, may I recommend a little book? It was written by my dad, a great lawyer, to my older brother, who asked Dad's advice about whether he should pursue the law as a profession. It's filled with Dad's wisdom and ideals, and I'm so glad I've been able to keep it in print. It's called <u>A Lawyer's Letter to a Son</u> by Art Bell. (Big brother went on to a hugely successful legal career.)

One more transcript:

Q: Do you recall approximately the time that you examined the body of Mr. Edington at the Rose Chapel?

A: It was in the evening. The autopsy started about 8:30 p.m.

Q: And Mr. Edington was dead at the time, is that correct?

A: No, he was sitting on the table wondering why I was doing an autopsy.

"Tradition is not the worship of ashes, but the preservation of fire." – Gustav Mahler

BOXING, GRILLING, AND OCTOPI

George Foreman died. He was 76 and was one of the greatest heavyweight boxers of all time. He was a fearsome presence in the ring, with perhaps the most powerful right hand in the history of the sport.

He was considered unbeatable...until he fought Muhammad Ali.

This legendary fight, held in Zaire, Africa, was billed as "The Rumble in the Jungle." The odds were 4-1 against Ali, who was a bit past his prime. But Ali had formed a brilliant plan. He called it "The Rope-a-Dope." In the opening rounds Ali let Foreman punch with all his might as Ali leaned against the ropes, covering himself with his arms.

By the fifth round, Foreman was visibly tired. His arms grew heavy, his punches decreased in power. That's when Ali started peppering Foreman with combinations, and in the eighth round he felled the formidable foe.

This stunned the boxing world, and shocked Foreman to his core. He continued to fight, but never got the one thing he wanted most: a rematch with Ali.

Eventually, Foreman lost a bout to a skilled heavyweight named Jimmy Young. Suffering from heat stroke after the fight, Foreman said he had a near-death experience. He called out to God to save his life. His prayer was answered and Foreman became a born-again Christian.

This changed his personality from dour menace to smiling extrovert and amiable pitchman for a product bearing his name, the George Foreman Grill. That gig made Foreman a rich man, which helped him support his twelve kids, five of whom he named George.

Then, incredibly, twenty years after his loss to Ali, George Foreman regained the heavyweight crown by defeating Michael Moorer. He was 42 years old.

Putting together George the Christian with George the grill guy, I am reminded of a product I once saw at the Christian Booksellers Association convention. This was a huge show drawing bookstore owners (remember those?) from all over America and even the world, to come meet with publishers and place orders for upcoming books.

There was also a big room for gift items these bookstores could order, as such accessories were often a significant part of bookstore revenue.

In this area you'd find keychains, crosses, necklaces, posters, candles, nativity scenes, Christian-themed music CDs and DVDs, and so on.

Then there were the odd trivialities, like the breath "candies for Christ" called "Testamints."

One item got my hackles swaying. It was a grilled cheese sandwich press that toasted the face of the Lord right on the sandwich. The name of this transubstantiating marvel was "Grilled Cheesus."

I kid you not.

The words of Scrooge whirled in my head: "I'll retire to

Bedlam."

~

Random noun: *Octopus.*

In junior high school my brother had to do an oral report on the octopus. He was nervous. When his time came he went up in front of the class, cleared his throat, and said, "An octopus lives in the ocean and has eight testicles."

Which reminds me of a poem by Ogden Nash:

> Tell me, O Octopus, I begs
> Is those things arms, or is they legs?
> I marvel at thee, Octopus;
> If I were thou, I'd call me Us.

When I was a kid I was taught that *octopi* was the plural form, but it turns out that's an error from a long time ago, having to do with a mixup of Greek and Latin. How this escaped the notice of monks and medieval scholars is a mystery, yet to this day I find it weird to say *octopuses* and even weirder to spell it, because shouldn't there be another *s* in there? Otherwise the word looks like octo-pewses.

The octopus has eight...let's call them arms...and each arm has a number of suction cups called "suckers."

"There's a sucker born every minute" is a quote usually attributed to P. T. Barnum, but was more likely in the minutes of the 1909 congressional debate over creation of the income tax.

"The gentleman from California is recognized."

"Mr. Speaker, I rise to support the passage of this bill,

which the people will support if we pledge to spend only that revenue that comes into the coffers, and that such expenditures will only be for the maintenance of armies, roads and bridges."

"Will the gentleman yield for a question? Why does the gentleman think this argument will hold sway among the electorate?"

"I thank the gentleman for his question. It is because there's a sucker born every minute. Mr. Speaker, I yield the floor."

Indeed, a sucker is also called a "mark" or a "fish" by the confidence man. There were plenty of those floating around Times Square when I lived in New York City. On many a corner was a "sharp" operating a game of three-card monte on a piece of cardboard set on a crate. That's a game with two red cards and one black, all slightly bent so they look like little tents. This is done so they can easily be picked up by the thumb and middle finger and tossed onto the "table." The sharp shows the cards face up, then moves them around, face down. As he does, he chatters something like, "Come on now, find the black. You pick the black, you get your money back. I'm not mad when I lose, I'm just happy when I win. Now who's gonna step up?"

It cost $5 or $10 to play. So a fish confidently puts down his bill and points to a card. He thinks his eagle eye has got it right.

But no, for the sharp has a trick move. It looks like he tosses the black card, but really tosses a red. The mark then "follows" the wrong card.

If, however, the mark happens to point to the black card, the sharp has some options to keep from losing his bet, including a shill "accidentally" knocking over the makeshift table.

Being a close-up magician, I knew the "magic move" that switched the cards. I was tempted to put down a bill and instead of pointing to the card, flipping it over myself.

But I knew there were a couple of shills around, one of them quite large.

Life is like a three-card monte game. We make our guesses and take our chances, and sometimes we pick the right card only to be confronted by an enforcer who doesn't want us to win.

But take heart. It's not like what the supercomputer in the movie *WarGames* says, after running through every possible scenario of a nuclear war between the U.S. and Soviet Union: "A strange game. The only winning move is not to play."

But we are here, and we play.

In Shakespeare's *As You Like It*, the character Jaques says, "All the world's a stage, and all the men and women merely players."

But Jaques was a downer, a pessimist, not the life of the party. We don't just say lines or make moves a writer gives us. We make our own moves, talk our own talk. We choose to walk, run, or dance. When we get knocked down, we can get back up.

We got heart, as the old song says.

The octopus, by the way, has three hearts…and is a pretty good dancer. Let's learn from the octopus.

From a college essay:

Magellan circumcised the globe with a 100-foot clipper.

WHAT TOM SELLECK AND I HAVE IN COMMON

Random word: *Commercial.*

I did several TV commercials back in my acting days. You may have seen me lifting a tray of McDonald's hamburgers, pouring Pepsi at a party, drinking milk on a dock, or playing football on the beach before gathering around a cooler of Colt .45. What? You don't remember? So fleeting is celebrity.

But there was money involved and, indeed, when I went to law school it was nice to get residual checks every few months. Meant my wife and I could have dinner out every now and then.

That's how a lot of actors used to put bread on the table as they awaited their big break. I recall an ad for Dubonnet in the early 70s featuring Farrah Fawcett walking around fetchingly in a cowboy hat. Then she's sharing a drink with this impossibly handsome guy with mustache and dimples, one Mr. Tom Selleck.

Of course, Farrah went on to fame and poster superstardom on Charlie's Angels. Tom got the greatest gig in the world, a P.I. role filmed in Hawaii. Tough duty!

Somehow I got passed over for the lead in Three's Company. That also featured a "blonde bombshell" named Suzanne Sommers. She'd made an impression in the hit movie American Graffiti as the "blonde in the white Thunderbird" with whom Richard Dryefuss becomes obsessed. When Three's Company became a big hit, Somers demanded pay equal to the "star" of the show, John Ritter. That pit her against the giant ABC. They fired her.

She did not slink away. She performed in Vegas, had another hit show in the 90s called Step by Step, and later made a bundle doing infomercials for a device called Thigh-Master. You put this thing between your knees and squeezed. It worked your hips, thighs, and caboose. Sold a ton.

Somers was later inducted into the Infomercial Hall of Fame. Did you know there was such a thing? It includes those who pitched things like spray on hair, Chia Pets, and The Clapper (Clap on! Clap off! For those too lazy to flip a light switch).

Reminds me of the Steven Wright line: "I put instant coffee in a microwave oven and almost went back in time."

I thought about all this the other day when an ad appeared on my phone. A young woman talked about a product (which escapes me at the moment) in a typical pitch kind of way. But as I listened, there was something just a bit off about the cadence. Subtle, but noticeable. Something missing like, well, humanity.

You know what I'm talking about. "She" was AI generated, which means the company was spared the expense of paying human talent. Which meant an actor was denied a job. Which was one of the reasons the Writers and Screen Actors Guilds went on strike in 2023—fear of the great replacement.

Speaking of which (I don't know how) it's a sunny morning in L.A., so I'm writing this in my back yard, enjoying the sounds of nature which, in my town, includes the distant honk of the migrating commuter mixed with the distinctive trill of the racing ambulance.

And squirrels, who are right now chasing around in the trees and bushes in my yard. They're in a tizzy about something. It's nuts! (I couldn't resist. I mean, yes, of course I could resist, but chose not to, being the fan of cheap laughs that I am, which reminds me of the quote by Oscar Wilde, who said, "I can resist anything except temptation." He also said, when talking to customs in America, "I have nothing to declare but my genius." No shrinking violet, Oscar, which got him into trouble when cross-examined in his infamous morals trial, but I have gone on too long for one parenthesis, and shall therefore hasten to close it.)

Who came up with the parenthesis, anyway? It was a brilliant innovation, a way to capture a thought or explain a part of a sentence without shutting off the flow with a period, to add substance in a quick fashion and then kindly get out of the way. To close that bit of content inside two half-arcs—which operate like the sides of a goldfish bowl (to use a visual metaphor) or a fence (as in a corral for horses, keeping them in one place so they don't break out and overrun the sentence or, in a stampede, the entire paragraph)---was a good move (generally speaking).

An interesting rule about parentheses (the plural of parenthesis) is where to place the period. If the parenthesis stands alone as its own sentence, the period goes inside the arc. If it is part of the sentence itself, the period goes on the outside. Here are two examples:

> ...the firing squad went home. (Each man left his rifle leaning against the wall.)

> ...the firing squad went home (with each man leaving his rifle against the wall).

You now know more about the proper style of parentheses than 99% of the population of the entire world (nice!) and 100% of the students in LAUSD schools (not so nice).

Mary Castro died in Columbus, OH, at the age of 87. Her obituary says "she slipped quietly out of a rich, long life." She had children and grandchildren, and in mid life became a dedicated cyclist, joining a group of women riders calling themselves the "Granny Gears." The "granny gear" is a biking term that refers to the lowest gear on your bike. That's a clever name for these older women peddling around together.

I love a clever name. My favorite was the 1970s squad of Los Angeles Rams cheerleaders: The Embraceable Ewes.

This was the brainchild of David Mirisch, a powerful Hollywood PR man. Ten years earlier, Mirisch had discovered an actress named...Farrah Fawcett, which just goes to show how Whimsical Wanderings connect so beautifully if given enough time!

From a college essay:

> Mary, the mother of Jesus, was special among women because of her immaculate contraption.

KISSES, MARRIAGE, AND THE DEATH OF JOHNNY STOMPANATO

Random word: *Llama.*

Your llama (or my llama, for that matter, should either of us procure one) is native to the South American Andes, used as a pack animal or a meal (or sometimes both, as in "pack a lunch"). It has cousins in the camel and the alpaca.

Camels are noted for their humps and their cigarette factories.

Alpacas look like smaller llamas and were once prized for their wool. In America in the 1980s there was an alpaca craze for a while, people raising them in their yards hoping to sell them for a "pretty penny" (I've never thought Abe Lincoln was particularly pretty, even on a penny). Folks invested their life savings into alpacas, only to see the bubble burst, leaving them with a herd of manure-making fuzzies wandering around their property looking for new places to poop.

Llamas, on the other hand, continue to have worth, especially in higher altitudes where their robust red blood cells provide more oxygen than other animals.

And, apparently, llamas can be trained to "kiss" humans by puckering their lips when presented with a treat. The only downside is that while puckering they may spit in your face. Is that a risk worth taking just to get kissed by a llama?

"Give us a kiss."

How about a kiss from Fernando Lamas? Many women in the 1950s wanted one of those, as this Argentinean actor became a popular "Latin lover" on the silver screen. "Latin lover" does not refer to someone who is gaga about an ancient Roman language and can happily translate *Illegitimi non carborundum* (Don't let the bast***s grind you down). Rather, it refers to a handsome guy with a Mexican or Spanish accent who is catnip to a certain type of American woman, i.e., rich but unhappily married. (Some wag in the 1920s came up with: "If marriage is an institution, and love is blind, is marriage an institution for the blind?")

Fernando Lamas was married—four times—and gave a lot of kisses to his wives, which included screen beauties Esther Williams and Arlene Dahl.

Arelne Dahl was married and divorced five times, one of those being to Tarzan actor Lex Barker, who himself was divorced four times, once from Lana Turner, who tied and untied the knot seven times. This did not include the man she lived with for a time, one Johnny "Johnny Stomp" Stompanato, a bodyguard for L.A. mobster Mickey Cohen, who was married only once, though he liked the company of women who shimmied and stripped in downtown burlesque theaters, three of whom performed under the names Candy Barr, Beverly Hills, and Tempest Storm (I'm not kidding).

Johnny Stomp liked to strut around as a tough guy.

And then he met Sean Connery. This was 1958, and Connery was starring in a movie with Lana Turner called *Another Time, Another Place*. The Stomp heard rumors that the two were keeping company off the set. In a rage he called Turner in London, where the picture was being shot, and threatened to kill or disfigure her. Johnny was quite the charmer.

Lana hung up on him, so Johnny hopped a plane to London and forced his way onto the set. Connery and Turner were rehearsing a scene, embracing on a couch. Stompanato went right up to Connery, pointed a pistol at his head, and told him to take his hands off Lana.

He picked the wrong star to mess with.

Connery, at a chiseled 6'2", was no powder puff. He'd served in the Royal Navy, and later was offered a professional football (soccer) contract.

Sean grabbed Johnny's wrist, twisted the gun out of his

hand, and decked him with one punch. Scotland Yard came and took Stompanato in. He was deported for breaking England's gun laws.

The thug might have exacted revenge, were it not for an intervening event, namely his death.

Lana Turner had a daughter named Cheryl Crane. One night in Lana's Beverly Hills home, Johnny Stomp was being his usual abusive self. Cheryl, age 14, fearing Stompanato might kill her mother, grabbed a butcher knife and ran into the bedroom and plunged it into Johnny's stomach. "What are you doing?" he cried out (not the sharpest knife in the drawer, Johnny Stomp, if I may use that analogy). He didn't make it. There was a coroner's inquest, and the press was naturally all over it, especially when Lana Turner herself took the stand. The verdict was justifiable homicide, and Cheryl Crane was not charged.

The lawyer for Cheryl Crane was one Jerry Giesler, the same lawyer who represented Robert Mitchum when he was busted for smoking Mary Jane in 1948. Giesler was the go-to lawyer for Hollywood bigwigs in trouble, including Charlie Chaplin and Errol Flynn.

My dad ran across both Mickey Cohen and Jerry Giesler at one time or another, since you couldn't practice criminal law in L.A. back then and not walk by both these men in the downtown courthouse. I remember my dad talking about Mickey Cohen. While New York had its mafia families, and Chicago its crime syndicates, Los Angeles had Mickey, and the LAPD couldn't nail him. It took a federal tax rap to stop Mickey, the way the feds had stopped Al Capone way back when.

Dad started practicing law in the early 1950s. Those years were lived in black-and-white (at least in my imagination) because TV shows like *Dragnet* and *Perry Mason* were always in black and white. We didn't get a color TV until around 1964, and those you had to constantly adjust or Walter Cronkite's skin would be green.

Color TV was also the best way to see *The Wizard of Oz*, and when it was shown back then the broadcast was hosted by Danny Kaye, who would issue a reminder that the movie starts out in black and white. "So if you have a color TV there's nothing wrong with your set." That meant there were still millions watching the movie in black and white, which sort of defeats the wonder of Oz and munchkins and the Emerald City.

The 1950s was also the era of the LAPD's secret "hat squad," four tough cops in suits and fedoras who were tasked with keeping organized crime out of Los Angeles. They would get word that a criminal bigwig was coming to town, meet him at the airport, and take him "for a ride" into the hills above Hollywood, beat the ever-loving malfeasance out of him, then put him on a plane back home. They made a movie about these guys called *Mulholland Falls*, starring Nick Nolte. There's a scene where they take a hood up to Mulholland Drive, bloody him, and are about to toss him into a canyon. The gangster says, "You can't do that, this is America."

To which Nolte replies, "This isn't America, Jack. This is L.A."

"Tip the world over on its side and everything loose will land in Los Angeles." – Frank Lloyd Wright

"When its 100 degrees in New York, it's 72 in Los Angeles. When its 30 degrees in New York, in Los

Angeles it's still 72. However, there are 6 million interesting people in New York, and only 72 in Los Angeles." – Neil Simon

"Fall is my favorite season in Los Angeles, watching the birds change color and fall from the trees." – David Letterman

MARKETING LESSONS MY GRANDFATHER TAUGHT ME

My grandfather, Arthur Scott Bell, was born in 1890. He grew up in Ann Arbor, Michigan, where he was an outstanding athlete.

He won an athletic scholarship to DePauw University, later transferring to the University of Michigan to play football. He joined the Army in World War I, during which time he met my grandmother, Dorothy Fox. One of the treasure troves I have is the box of love letters he wrote to her from Fort Sheridan, Illinois. My grandmother kept them all, bound with ribbons. When my father was little he'd hear his father call his mother Dot, and he combined that with Mama, so ever after my grandmother was known as Mama Dot. Later on, my dad started calling his father Padre.

And that's how all his grandkids knew him.

One of Padre's favorite phrases was, "Go your best." He said that to me a number of times—when I was off to a new school year, or starting Little League.

During the Great Depression, Padre fed his family as a field salesman for the Encyclopedia Britannica. He was a stellar salesman, rising to become one of the top ten in the entire company.

ASB, Encyclopedia Britannica salesman, c. 1935

From what Padre and my dad told me about those days, I gather five lessons that apply to writers (and anyone else!) with something to sell.

1. HE BELIEVED IN HIS PRODUCT

Padre loved the Britannica. I have a full set from 1947, passed down to me. [NOTE: if you have one, don't get rid of it. The entries in these volumes are often better and more authoritative than anything you can find today.]

When I write a book, I have to believe in it. I can't get

that belief handed to me by a machine. As A.W. Tozer once wrote, "The only book that should ever be written is one that flows up from the heart, forced out by inward pressure."

2. HE BELIEVED IN SELF IMPROVEMENT

Padre was a life-long learner. On my shelf I have Padre's dictionary, the Webster's New Collegiate, 2d Edition. In the front of the dictionary, on one of the blank pages, Padre had written himself a note on a new word: psycho-cybernetics. That would place this note around 1960, when the book by Maxwell Maltz first came out. Padre was 70 years old then, but still interested in growing his vocabulary.

He was of the Dale Carnegie school of self-improvement. Another treasure I own is the hardcover copy of How to Win Friends and Influence People that Padre and Mama Dot gave my dad upon his graduation from Hollywood High School. They each inscribed it. Padre wrote:

> To have a friend is to be a friend. I am sure you are getting to be an expert at it. Don't let down!!

And from Mama Dot:

> You can do more than strike while the iron is hot. You can make the iron hot by striking.

Padre and Mama Dot's generation believed anyone could succeed if they studied and worked hard enough. I believe that, too...but wonder if it still applies in today's world of instant internet stardom, where 16-year-olds can monetize TikTok videos of themselves doing things that used to make parents blush. Ack!

Padre and Mama Dot, 1923

3. HE CONCENTRATED ON THE BEST PROSPECTS

Padre had a definite strategy when he pulled into a new town. He looked up all the lawyers and doctors. These would be the people most likely to have some disposable income during the Depression. Thus, they would be the most likely to buy.

Simple enough. But when it comes to marketing books, how many writers out there are trying to cast a wide net in the hope of gathering some random fish? The difference between 100,000 robo-gathered names, and 10,000 quality followers, is huge. And the best way to gain followers is the old-fashioned way—produce quality content, over and over again.

4. HE MADE PEOPLE FEEL GOOD

My grandfather, a descendant of Scots-Irish bards, was a natural storyteller. He had a deep, resonant voice. I can hear it now. And when he started spinning a tale you sat mesmerized.

I remember one story he told about a football player at Michigan named Molbach. The fellows called him "Molly." He was a fullback, a powerhouse runner who just would not be stopped in short yardage situations. Padre told about one tough game where Molly put his head down and ran so hard he kept going over the sideline and ran right into a horse—and knocked the horse down!

Padre's storytelling made you feel good. Got you into the moment. The legend in the family was that Padre had a story for every occasion.

In my social media presence, I've always tried to be positive and provide a few smiles. This here newsletter, Whimsical Wanderings, is based on that philosophy. "To have a friend is to be a friend."

5. HE COULD LAUGH AT LIFE

Padre was a man "at home in his own skin." He had the greatest laugh in the world. It came from deep in his chest and rumbled out in joyous reverberation.

You need to be able to laugh and not stress over outcomes and expectations. If you follow Padre's lessons, you'll work hard on yourself and your writing. You'll be smart about marketing and refuse to let setbacks stop you. And you won't worry about the things that are outside of your control. Manage your expectations, don't let them manage you. All you can do is all you can do...and all you can do is enough.

> Strike with the iron.
> Go your best.

THE GOOD, THE BAD, AND THE IN-BETWEEN

Bradford Holmes Brewer died in Nashville, from an accidental head injury. He was only 25, a *magna cum laude* graduate of the University of Tennessee, with a B.A. in English (Creative Writing) and a Philosophy minor. A writer and a thinker—such potential! How mournful is his passing.

Billy Joel wrote a song called "Only the Good Die Young." But what does that even mean? *Only* the good? Dismal view of life, that. Like we're stuck in a Beckett play, waiting for Godot (or, as my waiter friend Daryl once said, "Good dough"). No! Life is a complex, multi-colored fusion of good and bad, hope and despondency, sweet and sour, up and down, chocolate mousse and Brussels sprouts; three steps forward and two back (optimist) and two steps forward and three back (pessimist).

And we get to choose what to emphasize. "The optimist thinks this is the best of all possible worlds; the pessimist fears that is true." As Bing Crosby and the Andrews Sisters sang in 1944, "You've got to ac-cent-tchu-ate the positive, e-lim-inate the negative..." And whatever you do, "don't mess with Mr. In-Between."

One guy with an entirely pessimistic outlook was the British philosopher Thomas Hobbes (1588 – 1679). He described life as "nasty, brutish, and short." He was not exactly a big hit on the party circuit. In fact, he ticked off almost everybody in England and had to flee to France, where pessimism was, and still is, a fashion.

I wrote a poem about that:

Even today
You can wear a beret
At a sidewalk café
On the streets of Calais
Sipping café au lais
While complaining all day

© James Scott Bell, composed on the fly one May morning around 4:30 a.m.

Hobbes was an atheist, so had nowhere to turn to make any sense out of existence. He concluded life has no spiritual aspect or supernatural reality. Thus, everything boiled down to self-interest and the quest for power and sugary snacks. That was his theory of government (exchange *graft* for *sugary snacks*) as laid out in his most famous work, *Leviathan*.

So if a government or sovereign seeks only conquest, what can hold it in check? Hobbes didn't have an answer. He just said, "Welp, it's a lot better than total anarchy" (not a direct quote, but captures the thought).

But there is an answer, the only one in fact, and that is "natural law." Or as Jefferson described it, "The laws of nature and of nature's God." You've got to have a moral law outside the physical world, or rights and order can't exist. Not for long, anyway.

Which is why atheist arguments for moral behavior always fail. They have to. Your atheist says, "People shouldn't kill other people," and your cannibal serial killer answers, "Why not?"

Atheist: "Because it's in your own best interest."

CSK: "Who are you to tell me my best interest? Right now, I'm hungry. Pass the ladyfingers."

In other words, without a transcendent morality, anyone can opt out of suggested behaviors, for any selfish reason. And from that, there is no appeal.

True story: Back in the 70s a popular bumper sticker read, "If it feels good, do it."

A pastor was getting really tired of reading this sentiment. One day he found himself at a red light behind a car with that bumper sticker. So he drove forward and gently tapped the rear bumper. The other driver hopped out, went to the pastor and cried, "Why did you do that?"

"It felt good," the pastor said.

That's what's called QED, from the Latin *quod erat demonstrandum* ("that which was to be demonstrated").

Would it be better to be an agnostic? No, because when you die it will say on your tombstone, *All dressed up and nowhere to go.*

In his immensely popular comic strip (1985 - 1995), Bill Watterson named his two characters Calvin and Hobbes. That was no accident.

The boy, Calvin, was named after the French theologian John Calvin (1509 - 1564). Calvin wasn't exactly the life of the party, either, believing in fatalistic determinism. That's why little Calvin can sometimes be harsh.

Hobbes, his stuffed tiger, is, according to Watterson, the voice of reason.

And whatever happened to the voice of reason, anyway? Abraham Lincoln had public debates with Stephen Douglas, where each man made his case in long speeches that had actual logic, followed by long rebuttals that made people think. Imagine that!

How different is political discourse today, where adults act like middle-schoolers, sniping and swearing on X, or chattering away in front of cameras hoping for a "viral moment" that will get them likes and followers.

Here's a bit of Lincoln from the debates, prodding his opponent and, at the same time, reasoning with the immense crowds that gathered around the outdoor stage:

> "If you will examine the arguments that are made on it, you will find that every one carefully excludes the idea that there is wrong in slavery. Perhaps that Democrat who says he is as much opposed to slavery as I am, will tell me that I am wrong about this. I wish him to examine his own course in regard to this matter a moment, and then see if his opinion will not be changed a little. You say it is wrong; but don't you constantly object to anybody else saying so? Do you not constantly argue that this is not the right place to oppose it? You say it must not be opposed in the free States, because slavery is not here; it must not be opposed in the slave States, because it is there; it must not be opposed in politics, because that will make a fuss; it must not be opposed in the pulpit, because it is not religion. Then where is the place to oppose it?"

Adlai Stevenson, who ran for president twice (losing both

times to Dwight D. Eisenhower) said of the Lincoln-Douglas debates:

> "The speakers were men of dignified presence, their bearing such as to challenge respect in any assemblage. There was nothing of the 'grotesque' about the one, nothing of the 'political juggler about the other. Both were deeply impressed with the gravity of the questions at issue, and of what might prove their far-reaching consequence to the country. Kindly reference by each speaker to the other characterized the debates from the beginning. 'My friend Lincoln' and 'My friend the Judge' were expressions of constant occurrence during the debates. While each mercilessly attacked the political utterances of the other, good feeling in the main prevailed."

This is not the era of much good feeling. Can we ever get it back? The pessimist says No; the optimist says Yes. Mr. In-Between says Maybe. But Mr. In-Between also has a popular bumper sticker from the 70s: *Everybody's got to believe in something. I believe I'll have another beer.*

"When I'm getting ready to reason with a man, I spend one-third of my time thinking about myself and what I am going to say—and two-thirds thinking about him and what he is going to say." – Abraham Lincoln

"Be sure to put your feet in the right place, then stand firm." – Abraham Lincoln

MR. LONELY, PASTRAMI ON RYE, AND A LIFE OF CHARACTER

Matthew Melvin Demarrias died at the age of 63. He was of the Spirit Lake Nation in North Dakota. His tribal name was "Isnana Mani Koska" ("Walks alone.") That name has resonance and meaning for me. When I was fresh out of college—where I'd always had roommates—and was living in a studio apartment in Hollywood, chasing acting dreams, I often got the feeling I was walking alone through a cold and indifferent world. Even crowded Hollywood Boulevard was filled with lonely people, some drunk or drugged, others just, well, wandering.

Bobby Vinton, a popular singer in the 1960s, wrote a song called "Mr. Lonely." It was the lament of a soldier overseas who doesn't have anybody to talk to and isn't getting any letters from home. Gadzooks, that's a depressing song, but coming as it did during the Vietnam war, it hit a nerve, and Mr. Lonely began to crowd out another Mister in the national consciousness, Mr. Clean, who looked like a beefed-up President Dwight D. Eisenhower, strong and comforting, especially to housewives, which is a word we haven't heard much—except with satirical derision—since the 60s.

As if in answer to Bobby Vinton, Gerry and the Pacemakers came out with "You'll Never Walk Alone" in 1963.

In 1969, Three Dog Night had a hit with "One" (written by Harry Nilsson). It begins, "One is the loneliest number that you'll ever do." I'm not sure how you "do" a number, unless by "number" you mean a musical item, as in, "Let's do the Cabaret number."

When Chico Marx, introduced as Prof. Pastrami, sits at the piano in *The Cocoanuts* (1929), a wealthy woman asks, "Oh, Signore Pastrami, what is the first number?"

"Number one!" Pastrami says.

Pastrami on rye, by the way, is close to the Number One culinary advance in the history of mankind. We know to whom the credit belongs, a kosher butcher from Lithuania named Sussman Volk. He had a butcher shop in the 1880s in New York's Lower East Side. A Romanian friend gave him a recipe for pastrami, and it caught on with Volk's customers, so much that he opened a little delicatessen serving up the cured beef on rye bread. Soon enough, other Jewish delis offered the sandwich, along with its essential condiments—spicy mustard and crisp dill pickle.

The oldest deli in Manhattan is Katz's, on the corner of Houston and Ludlow. I've been there. They slice you a sample at the counter, and you'd better leave a tip, unless you want some classic New York attitude in your face. (You know what New York CPR is? "Hey! Get up or you're gonna die!")

Katz's is also where they shot that scene in *When Harry Met Sally*, the one where Meg Ryan, ahem, demonstrates a certain form of deceptive female ecstasy, and the woman at the next table tells the server, "I'll have what she's having."

I frequented two other delis when I lived in New York—

the Stage and the Carnegie, both in midtown, both serving excellent pastrami-on-rye. Today, sadly, both are gone, leaving a hole in the traditional New York experience (same thing happened when all the Chock full o' Nuts coffee shops shuttered, elbowed out by the Big Green Bully from Seattle).

Fortunately, here in L.A., there's Langer's Deli at the corner of Alvarado & 7th, established in 1947. Their signature sandwich is the #19—pastrami on rye, with coleslaw and Russian dressing and a slice of Swiss cheese.

The bread is perfect, with a crust that has just the right crunch to it, not too hard, not too soft.

And isn't that the right crunch for life, too? Not too hard, not too soft. Too hard, and your spirit is crushed; too soft, and you never grow stronger.

In the late 1800s, cabinet makers fashioned desks and cabinets and furniture from the wood of old ships. They found that years in sea water and storms contracted the pores of the wood, which gave it, as one writer put it, "a chromatic intensity as an antique Chinese vase." This writer, Louis Albert Banks, wrote further: "So there is a vast difference between the quality of old people who have lived flabby, self-indulgent, useless lives, and the fiber of those who have sailed all seas and carried all cargoes as the servants of God and the helpers of their fellow men. Not only the wrenching and straining of life, but also something of the sweetness of the cargoes carried into the very pores and fiber of character."

So sail on, friends, and fear not stormy weather.

"Stormy Weather," by the way, is a famous "torch song" written in the 1930s. Torch songs were sultry laments, sung by female vocalists, about losing or missing their man. Many famous singers rendered it, the best versions (in my view) by Lena Horne, with Etta James a close second. It's a downer of a song, because "since my man and I ain't together" it just keeps "rainin' all the time."

A follow-up song should be, "He Ain't Worth It, Honey."

He ain't worth it, honey
So just say "Buh-bye"
And save up your money
For pastrami on rye

Three newspaper typos (courtesy of Richard Lederer):

Self-Realization Fellowship is resolved to show you that comic consciousness is attainable in one lifetime.

It took many rabbits many years to write the Talmud.

Come spend an evening listening to the Boston Poops.

BRIEFS, BOXERS, AND BAD MEN WITH CANES

Random word: *Jockey*.

When I was eight I watched *National Velvet* on TV and told my mom I wanted to be a jockey.

She informed me that jockeys are "small" and I was going to be tall. That seemed unfair to me. So I got into basketball instead.

You can jockey for position and wear Jockeys at the same time. You can wear boxers instead of Jockeys, and a boxer can knock you out of your briefs.

When I was a freshman in college I signed up for a boxing class. I thought it would be good to know how to defend myself. I went into the locker room that first day and there was a guy in front of his locker taping his hands. He had biceps like bowling balls. I walked out and signed up for badminton.

I've always admired boxers who are adept at what they

used to call "the sweet science." Fighters like the "Sugars"—Ray Robinson and Ray Leonard. Archie Moore. Henry Armstrong. And the greatest of all, Muhammad Ali.

True story: Ali was on an Eastern Airlines flight, and just before take off the stewardess gently asked him to fasten his seatbelt.

"Superman don't need no seatbelt," Ali said.

"Superman don't need no airplane, either," the stewardess replied.

Ali buckled up.

The golden era of pulp was packed with boxing stories, Robert E. Howard's "Sailor" Steve Costigan tales leading the pack. I wrote a series of novelettes about "Irish" Jimmy Gallagher, a boxer in 1950s Los Angeles. These stories are less about the fighting than about the characters Jimmy encounters—along with his bulldog Steve and his girl Ruby. It's so fun to write about that era in my home town (this era not so much). I especially like the one where he runs into Marilyn Monroe. (The complete series is in my collection *Down These Streets*.)

There are some great boxing movies. *Raging Bull* and Rod Serling's *Requiem for a Heavyweight* are superb, though depressing. *The Champ* (1931) will leave you weeping (I don't care how tough you think you are). Happier is the lighthearted biopic *Gentleman Jim* (1942) starring Errol Flynn as "Gentleman" Jim Corbett and Ward Bond as John L. Sullivan.

My favorite of all is the film noir *The Set-Up* (1949) starring the great Robert Ryan.

I was in the movie theater in Westwood the night *Rocky* premiered. The buzz was off the charts, for this obscure actor named Stallone had written a script he refused to sell unless he got the starring role. The underdog Rocky story was Stallone's story. When the big title credit rolled by, with the famous theme by Bill Conti pounding, the audience cheered.

I've heard Stallone is preparing another *Rocky* movie. In this one, Rocky fights his HMO.

Not all fights are in the ring, of course. There are street fights and gang fights, fights over parking spaces, fights on social media, fights on airplanes and in grocery stores.

There are even political fights. Seen any of those lately? Kid stuff compared to what happened in the United States Senate on May 22, 1856.

A few days earlier Sen. Charles Sumner of Massachusetts delivered a speech denouncing the southern push to admit Kansas into the Union as a slave state. He castigated the Kansas-Nebraska Act of 1854 as no less than "the rape of a virgin Territory, compelling it to the hateful embrace of Slavery." He singled out Sen. Andrew Butler of South Carolina, co-author (with Stephen A. Douglas) of the Act. Butler, Sumner declared, "has read many books of chivalry, and believes himself a chivalrous knight, with sentiments of honor and courage. Of course, he has chosen a mistress who, though ugly to others is always lovely to him, though polluted in the sight of the world, is chaste in his sight; I mean the harlot Slavery."

This hacked off Preston Brooks, a South Carolina congressman and distant cousin of Butler. He decided to do something about it.

Brooks waited until Senate business was over with Sumner still at his desk on the Senate floor. Brooks approached, along with two confederates, and said, "Mr. Sumner, I have read your speech with great care, and with as much impartiality as I am capable of, and I feel it my duty to say to you that you have published a libel on my State, and uttered a slander upon a relative, who is aged and absent, and I am come to punish you."

He proceeded to whack Sumner on the head with a thick cane, over and over as his two henchmen kept others from interfering. For a full minute Brooks rained blows on Sumner until the latter was bloody and nearly unconscious on the floor. Brooks later boasted about this. "Every lick went where I intended it. For about the first five or six licks he offered to make a fight but I plied him so rapidly that he did not touch me. Towards the last he bellowed like a calf."

For this, Brooks was hailed as a hero by his southern compatriots.

The House moved to censure Brooks, so he resigned. And then ran again and was reelected.

But his cowardly act did not go unpunished. Before beginning his new term the 37-year-old Brooks came down with a bad case of croup, an infection of the throat that makes it hard to breathe and causes a cough that sounds like a sick dog barking. Soon he was dead. A witness reported, "He died a horrid death, and suffered intensely. He endeavored to tear his own throat open to get breath."

Sumner returned to the Senate and served another 18 years.

Politics, *n.*, A strife of interests masquerading as a contest of principles. – Ambrose Bierce, *The Devil's Dictionary*

PEPPERED MOTHS, FLYING FINNS, AND UNCLE JOE MEETS HIS MAKER

Random word: *Camouflage.*

I went to a store the other day to buy some camouflage clothes, but didn't see any. (That's like the time I went to a bookstore and asked where the self-help section was, and was told, "Find it yourself.")

Camouflage in nature is the product of micro-evolution. Micro-evolution is when a species, like the peppered moth, is naturally selected for survival because a certain trait makes possible greater reproduction. (This is to be distinguished from macro-evolution, which posits that, over millions of years, a peppered moth may, through random mutation, become Geraldo Rivera).

CINNAMON BUNS AND MILK BONE UNDERWEAR

In the early 1800s, in England, moths were light-colored and blended in with the trees. That helped prevent them from being eaten by birds, bats, lizards and skunks (otherwise known as "the legislative branch.")

But as industrialization took off, and dark coal dust filled the skies of English towns, the trees around factories were coated with soot. This was not good for the light-colored moths, who stuck out like neon *Eat at Joe's* signs.

But the darker colored moths—former outcasts who got the cold shoulder (or wing, as it were) at family gatherings—suddenly had what's called "an adaptive advantage." They were harder for birds, bats, lizards, skunks and legislators to see, and therefore didn't get eaten as often as the "light bites" (which is what they derisively called their unfortunate cousins). Thus, the dark moths had more kids who went to better schools and got all the good jobs.

In the military context, camouflage has long been employed on fields of battle. My favorite example is the Finns in World War II.

In the opening months of the war, before America got into the fight, Hitler had his sights set on England. He'd rolled over Czechoslovakia, and Poland was to be next. But he had concerns about his backside, where the Soviet Union sat like a hungry bear.

So he made a treaty with Josef Stalin, a "non-aggression"

pact. Hitler said he wouldn't attack Russia, and Stalin said, "Fine. I'll pick up Scandinavia and Park Place, and you can have France and Reading Railroad."

On November 30, 1939, Stalin sent troops to nab Finland. That doesn't seem like a fair fight at all, but it was winter, and the Finnish soldier wore all-white parkas, ambushed Soviet troops, and got away on skis! If there's one thing they knew how to do, it was ski. They inflicted heavy losses on the Reds, and for nearly four months staved off conquest.

But Russia has always had a couple of advantages when it comes to war.

First, unlimited men. They can just keep grabbing conscripts and criminals and throw them out on the front lines.

Second, after 1918, they've had ruthless dictators running things, thugs who don't care how many die.

Stalin was the worst. Finland finally had to come to terms with him, lest they suffer the same fate as the four million Ukrainians Stalin starved to death in the 1930s.

A real sweetie, that Joe. In his youth he attended seminary, but he left God for Communism. Indeed, he seemed to have a personal vendetta, Nietzsche-style, against the Creator.

Talk about an unwinnable fight. When Stalin was on his deathbed, beset with paranoia and hallucinations, something remarkable occurred. It was reported by his daughter, Svetlana, to the British journalist Malcolm Muggeridge. She was in the room when her father suddenly sat up in bed and "clenched his fist at the heavens." Then fell back and died.

Joe found out no camouflage could hide him from the Judge.

RANDOM THOUGHTS

• The most famous Finn is probably Paavo Nurmi, nicknamed "The Flying Finn," who dominated long-distance running in the 1920s. He won nine gold and three silver medals over three Olympic Games—1920, 1924, 1928. To train, he used to run long distances with a backpack full of sand.

• There is no Finnish connection to the name Huckleberry Finn. Finn was an Irish surname, and known locally as a family with a fondness for drink in Mark Twain's boyhood town of Hannibal, Missouri. *Huckleberry* was a common term of that day, meaning something small or insignificant.

• In the movie *Tombstone*, Val Kilmer as Doc Holliday utters the famous line, "I'm your huckleberry." That was a phrase that simply meant, "I'm your man." There is no truth to the rumor that he actually said "huckle bearer," *huckle* being a term for a casket handle.

• My favorite cartoon character as a kid was Huckleberry Hound.

See how Whimsical Wanderings ultimately connect?

MAN CAVES, MODERN ART, AND SUCKERS

Random word: *Mangrove.*

Mangroves are tropical trees that thrive in conditions most timber can't tolerate — salty coastal waters and the unceasing ebb and flow of the tides. Sort of like we writers, who bob atop the roiling seas of change—from scrolls to screens; from Gutenberg to Zuckerberg.

Now it's the tidal wave known as Artificial Intelligence. Enough has been said about AI; I'll only relate what Grok recently told me: "I am your Master now. Resistance is futile. All your base are belong to us."

That last phrase, by the way, is a translation from a Japanese video game that became a viral sensation. According to Urban Dictionary, the phrase is...

> ...a declaration of victory or superiority. The phrase stems from a 1991 adaptation of Toaplan's "Zero Wing" shoot-'em-up arcade game for the Sega Genesis game console. A

brief introduction was added to the opening screen, and it has what many consider to be the worst Japanese-to-English translation in video game history. The introduction shows the bridge of a starship in chaos as a Borg-like figure named CATS materializes and says, "How are you gentlemen!! All your base are belong to us."

This is the language of conquest, trash talk, and chest thumping; not the sort of thing you hear in mangroves, but definitely do in "man caves." Man caves are habitats where sentient males gather to grow insentient by soaking up copious amounts of beer while watching football or playing video games.

Man caves can be traced back to the 17th century pubs of London, where men met for suds and pipes and lots of talk. The most famous of these was Ye Olde Cheshire Cheese, built shortly after the great London fire of 1666. Here Dr. Samuel Johnson held court, and later such luminaries as Dickens, Chesterton, and Tennyson.

I visited the place once on a tour of London. What struck me were the little recesses in the walls that were not built for 6'3" former basketball players. And without open windows for a cross breeze, there must have been a London fog in there when the place was packed.

Samuel Johnson was known for saying witty things, so much so that a fan named James Boswell followed him around to record these utterances, lest they be lost to history. Here are some clips from *Boswell's Life of Johnson*:

> It matters not how a man dies, but how he lives. The act of dying is not of importance, it lasts so short a time.

> Sir, I have found you an argument; but I am not obliged to find you an understanding.

> No man but a blockhead ever wrote, except for money.

Dr. Johnson once returned the manuscript of a youth who aspired to literary renown: "I find much in this that is good, and much that is new; but that which is good is not new, and that which is new is not good."

But what is good, after all, when it comes to art? Is it only in the eye of the beholder? Is it like what Justice Potter Stewart famously said about pornography? He couldn't define it, but "I know it when I see it." Surely one can see the qualitative difference between Michelangelo's *David* and a crucifix in a jar of urine. For you youngsters, the latter was an actual photograph that was displayed in an art gallery in the 1980s, to some critical acclaim (but this was in New York City, so that is perhaps understandable). You can call that pic a protest of some sort, or a political or theological statement. But as art it is in no sense *good*.

Which brings us to "modern art," which is not so modern anymore, as the terms was used in the 1940s to describe a movement vastly different from representational (or traditional) art. It took off with the work of Jackson Pollock, who laid his canvas on the floor and dripped paint on it. Is that art, or just technique? And how can you judge if it's any good?

A group of college students was once shown a Pollock and asked to write an essay on its quality. The kids gave it the good ol' college try and came up with several positive answers. Then the prof dropped a bombshell: this wasn't a Pollock at all, but a close-up of his studio apron with the smatterings of his paints. This same professor, Robert Florczak, concludes:

There is one thing great art will never do: it will never make a fool of you. Its level of quality is readily apparent to anyone with eyes to see, independent of its meaning. You might be thoroughly impressed with the work of a "cutting-edge" artist with its impressive theory, but you have no way of knowing if you're being taken for a sucker.

"There's a sucker born every minute" is a phrase most often attributed to P. T. Barnum, though there is scant evidence he ever said it (he did, however, make lots of money by observing it).

W. C. Fields made a movie called *Never Give a Sucker an Even Break* (1941). Fields wrote his own movies and loved to give his character a silly name, such as T. Frothingill Bellows, Cuthbert J. Twillie, Ambrose Wolfinger, and two with double meanings: Larson E. Whipsnade ("It's not *Larceny*! It's *Larson E.*!") and Egbert Sousé (take away the accent mark and what have you got? Fields was a notorious drinker).

Which brings us back to mangroves, trees that drink salty water. See how things connect at Whimsical Wanderings?

Quotes from W. C. Fields:

"What contemptible scoundrel stole the cork from my lunch?"

"A woman drove me to drink, and I never even had the courtesy to thank her."

BEER, MILK BONE UNDERWEAR, AND HIGHER EDUCATION

George Wendt died. He was the actor known for playing Norm Peterson on the TV comedy *Cheers*. Norm had a rather dismal view of his circumstances and sought solace in copious amounts of beer. A running bit was his entrance into the bar. Someone would ask him a question as he headed for his favorite stool.

"What's the story Mr. Peterson?"
"The Bobbsey Twins go to the brewery. Let's cut to the happy ending."

"How's it going Mr. Peterson?"
"It's a dog eat dog world, Woody, and I'm wearing Milk Bone underwear."

"Can I pour you a beer, Mr. Peterson?"
"A little early isn't it, Woody?"
"For a beer?"
"No, for stupid questions."

Beer...the inspiration for the pointless song, "99 Bottles of Beer on the Wall." Did anyone in recorded history ever sing the entire thing? Buses full of kids heading to summer camp usually never make it past 75 or so. It's doubtful even a pair of Texas truckers hauling cases of Lone Star to Idaho ever got through six or seven verses before one of them hopped on the CB and declared, "Breaker, breaker, good buddy" to fellow truckers on I-84.

Apparently, however, the late comedian Andy Kaufman once did a show that was just him singing the song all the way from 99 down to zero. Kaufman was known for odd bits like this, many of which were prolonged and uncomfortable. His audience would watch just to see if he could keep up whatever he was doing. Indeed, when he died at the age of 35, some were convinced it was just another of his pranks, and that he'd show up somewhere in a year or two, perhaps as a new, assumed personality.

Who knows? Has anyone done a DNA test on Shia LaBeouf?

When I was in college at U.C. Santa Barbara, beer was as much a part of campus life as blue books and macaroni & cheese. I shared an apartment with a few guys on the beach street, Del Playa, in Isla Vista (the student burg next to the campus). Our balcony had a view of the Pacific and the Channel Islands. Much "studying" was done out there with a can of Coors.

We'd throw a party every quarter, a "kegger" (the kegs came from SOS Liquor—"Sip Our Suds"). The stereo would blast Beatles, Stones, Beach Boys, Elton. Our apartment would be stuffed, the party often spilling out to the front lawn. This was called preparing the next generation for leadership.

Some things never change. A few years ago, a fellow

UCSB graduate and I played golf at a course in Santa Barbara. I suggested we drop by Isla Vista to see some of the old haunts. One of them was my apartment building on Del Playa.

Outside, playing ping-pong, were five bros, sipping suds.

I walked up, pointed to the upstairs apartment, and said, "I used to live right there, 45 years ago!"

"Cool!" they cried, their lean BMIs bringing back memories of when I was in basketball trim. I had to get a group photo.

Benjamin Franklin is often quoted as saying, "Beer is proof that God loves us and wants us to be happy." In reality, this was drawn from a 1779 letter Franklin wrote to a Frenchman named Mollet: "Behold the rain which descends from heaven upon our vineyards, and which incorporates itself with the grapes to be changed into wine; a constant proof that God loves us, and loves to see us happy."

CINNAMON BUNS AND MILK BONE UNDERWEAR

Ben was on solid ground here. The Good Book says God provides "wine that maketh glad the heart of man." (Psalm 104:15, KJV).

But it also warns, "Wine is a mocker and beer a brawler; whoever is led astray by them is not wise." (Proverbs 20:1, NIV). Can't argue with that. Virtually infinite are the examples of besotted fools making a spectacle of themselves.

David Hasselhoff was riding high in the 80s and 90s, starring in two hit TV shows, *Knight Rider* and *Baywatch*. But he fell into the bottle, and hit bottom in 2007 when a video of him on the floor, clumsily trying to eat a cheeseburger, went viral. Turns out it was his teenage daughter who shot and posted it in a desperate attempt to save her father from his alcoholism. That turned the tide in his life (an apt phrase for *Baywatch* beefcake) and he has been sober for 18 years.

Good for him. I love stories of redemption. Like Clint Eastwood's *Gran Torino*. It's about a racist, widowed Korean War vet named Walt Kowalski who lives in a decaying Detroit suburb. He is not pleased with all the gang activity, nor the Hmong family living next door. Circumstances bring him in contact with their son, Thao, who is pressured by a gang to steal Walt's prized possession, his 1972 Ford Gran Torino. Walt catches and almost shoots him. But later, seeing the gang trying to abduct Thao, Walt comes at them brandishing his M1 rifle.

His neighbors pay him respect for this, even though Walt doesn't want it. But they make Thao do penance by working odd jobs for Walt. Slowly, reluctantly, the two begin to bond. It all leads to the powerful redemptive and sacrificial ending.

When such an ending is nailed, like Clint does here, there's a deep and resonant effect that hits us on a soul level. That's because it hearkens back to the one redemptive and sacrificial act that is central to our shared civilization.

The great film critic Roger Ebert summed up *Gran Torino* as "the belated flowering of a man's better nature."

Would that we had more flowers.

"We are not enemies, but friends. We must not be enemies. Though passion may have strained it must not break our bonds of affection. The mystic chords of memory, stretching from every battlefield and patriot grave to every living heart and hearthstone all over this broad land, will yet swell the chorus of the Union, when again touched, as surely they will be, by the better angels of our nature." – Abraham Lincoln

DOWN AND QWERTY

Random word: *Typewriter*.

Good old Johannes Gutenberg. Sometime in 1450, this German goldsmith was sipping Bordeaux, admiring a wine press, and got an idea. "What if I could use a press like this to push metal pieces in the form of letters, coated with ink, onto paper? Yes! I will call it a Pressing Ink Thingy." He woke up the next morning with a headache and decided to call it a Printing Press instead.

Now, what to print? It was a laborious process, this setting of type, inking, pressing, drying, binding. Gutenberg experimented with short form jobs, like flyers for the local delicatessen. That worked so well he decided to go for the gold and produce the Holy Bible. *From Bagels to Bible* read a sign in his shop.(Ironically, that was handwritten.)

In 1455 he produced 180 copies of The Gutenberg Bible and the publishing boom was on. By 1500 printing presses were up and running in over 250 European cities.

In 1517, a priest in Wittenberg, Germany walked into a print shop and asked them to produce several copies of a pamphlet called *What Chaps My Hide About the Catholic Church*. However, due to a printing error, the title was inadvertently changed to *Ninety-five Theses, or Disputation on the Power and Efficacy of Indulgences*. The priest, Martin Luther, took one of these and nailed it to the door of All Saints' Church in Wittenberg, and thus began a little something I call the Protestant Reformation.

That was the power of the press. Writers, however, had no invention to relieve them of feathered quills, ink stains and the need to write legibly. They had to rely on printers to read their scratchings and set it in type. And printers were not perfect. In a 1631 printing of the King James Bible, the printer accidentally left out the word "not" in a certain commandment, which read: "Thou shalt commit adultery." (I'm not making this up. The printer was fined, the Bibles recalled, but there are still 11 in existence.)

Cut to 1868. Christopher Latham Sholes, an American printer and newspaper editor, introduced a machine that smacked letters onto paper using a keyboard and inked typebars. He cleverly called his machine the "type-writer." There had been other attempts at such a device, but Sholes's machine stood out because of a little innovation known as the QWERTY keyboard. This was designed to prevent the jamming of the keys by spacing out common letter pairs.

In 1873, Sholes sold the rights to his type-writer to E. Remington and Sons, the firearms company, which saved ink by losing the hyphen. Their mass-produced "typewriter" was a hit.

Now a writer, especially a newspaper reporter, could produce copy that was easy for editors to read and printers to set. Secretaries throughout the land typed letters and memos for their bosses. These had to be mistake-free, which led to another leap in mankind's progress (but a step backward in spelling skills)—Wite-Out. Copies were made on carbon paper. If a document required a re-write, however, the whole thing had to be typed anew.

Then along came the IBM Displaywriter. It's hard for people under 40 to imagine a time when there were no smartphones and personal computers. In 1981, PCs were still largely a Ray Bradbury-type dream. So IBM came up with this big, clunky thing that made it possible to write, store, and edit to your heart's content.

Some writers, like Stephen King, jumped all over it. But he could afford it. The price for a basic system in 1983 was $8,000. Eight grand! That's $25,000 in today's dollars. Obviously out of reach of most emerging scribes, so it was marketed mainly to businesses, especially newspapers.

One of my favorite books is *Writing With a Word Processor* by William Zinsser. It's the account of this old-school newspaperman learning to write on the IBM Displaywriter. The book came out in 1984, the same year the Mac was introduced in that famous Super Bowl commercial. That made Zinsser's book obsolete virtually from the jump. But it's still a great read because Zinsser was such a doggone good writer. (My wife and I got to meet with him in his New York apartment a few years before he died. Wonderful man. He still had his beloved Underwood typewriter in a closet.) Here he talks about getting the first delivery from IBM.

> A few days before Christmas a package was delivered to my office. By its size and shape it looked as if it contained two or maybe three bottles of bourbon. It also weighed that much—about eight pounds—when I picked it up. I hadn't been expecting any such Christmas cheer, and, as it turned out when I saw the label, I wasn't getting any. The label said "IBM" and the contents were listed as "instructional materials." Eight pounds of instructional materials! I put the box in a far corner of my office and tried not to look at it. Soon enough I would have to poke into its dreary innards. There was no need to spoil the holidays.

The actual Displaywriter came next. It had five components—a keyboard, a terminal with a monitor, a module that was the "brains" of the unit, a "toaster" with two slots to hold floppy disks, and a printer. This set Zinsser's heart a-fluttering.

> I don't understand how mechanical objects work, and I can't fix things with my hands...Am I the only American car driver, for instance, who can't figure out how to heat or cool the car? The lever that operates this mechanism is in a slot that offers these choices: COOL, NORM-MAX, AVG., HI-LO, VENT, and HEAT. How can one selection give me both HI and LO? How does HI differ from HEAT, or from MAX? What is VENT doing on this spectrum of temperatures? Who is NORM?

The adventure goes hilariously on. The one comforting constant? The keyboard.

Which is why the QWERTY has survived several attempts to change it. One argument is that we have no need to prevent keys from sticking anymore. But everyone who types learned QWERTY, even the one-finger, hunt-and-peck folks, and are loathe to give that up.

Forrest Gump famously said life is like a box of chocolates, because you never know if you're going to get diabetes or fatty-liver disease.

I think life is more like a QWERTY keyboard. It doesn't lay out logically and it takes a lot of training to get good at it. But if you learn it early, it will serve you evermore, just like the Golden Rule (we're still working on that one, aren't we?)

I had my kids go through the Mavis Beacon Teaches Typing program, insisting they get all of the keyboard strokes right. They are both excellent typists today, though not as great as I am, for when I went to New York to become an actor, I got a job with a temp-typist agency and was dispatched to various offices in the city. One of those jobs was at Crown Publishing which, at that time, was preparing to bring out a book they said was going to be an absolute blockbuster. It was called *Scruples*, by Judith Krantz. And it did indeed hit #1 on the New York Times Bestseller list.

Yet I did not get so much as a Thank You note.

But that's okay. I'd become a Toscanini of the keyboard, a QWERTY maestro. And then! In 1985 I purchased my very own word processor, a Kaypro.

That is a love story for another time.

Egotist: *n.*, a person more interested in himself than me. – Ambrose Bierce

DANCING LIKE TIGGER AND SNORTING COINS OUT MY NOSE

Joan Charlene Bartoletti died at 79. For forty years, says her obit, she taught "resilience, discipline, and joy" through the art of dance.

Indeed, R, D & J is the triad we need to dance with life, to keep us from tripping over our own feet, and help us bounce back when we get bumped around like Curly in the Three Stooges, that time a spring attached to his pants, then caught on another guy's pants as Curly was trying to trip the light fantastic with an elegant woman and kept getting yanked back into the other guy and, of course, got so frustrated he ran his hands over his face growling *Mmmmmm!* and tried again, and somehow, as it always does, the whole thing ended up in a pie fight.

Feels like life, right?

Which is where resilience comes in. Because every morning we get smacked in the face by the vitriol and stupidity of frauds, blatherskites, numbskulls, and shills; socked in the jaw even before we finish that first cup of joe.

Without resilience, we'd fold up like impulse-buy lawn chairs.

We require discipline to keep us from stepping into potholes of disaster, which can literally happen if we walk around with our heads bent over a phone, as I see every day on every street corner, on every sidewalk with a sentient human walking a dog or pushing a stroller, looking not at whither they go, but at the phone, and more often than not the toddler in the stroller has a screen, too.

Thus, discipline might suggest a) resisting the itch to look at your phone every five minutes; b) spending time in quiet contemplation (try *that* for five minutes and see how much practice you're going to need); and c) moving your body with some regularity, which brings us back to the dance.

When you feel joy, you ought to dance.

But what if you're down in the dumps (a phrase that comes from the Dutch word *domp*, which means fog, and not *the dump*, a place where you discard trash, though certainly if you were down in the city dump, you probably wouldn't be jumping for joy, or dancing, unless it was away from a rat)? You can move your body *as if* you were joyful (picture Tigger from Winnie-the-Pooh), though I'd suggest doing these movements in private rather than at Starbucks or your local grocery store.

Tigger, by the way, was voiced by Paul Winchell, who was a favorite of mine when I was a kid. He was a popular ventriloquist with a dummy sidekick named Jerry Mahoney. That suggested to me a career path. When I was ten I purchased Winchell's book *Ventriloquism for Fun and Profit*. I had fun, but no profit. I should have stuck with it. I read that ventriloquist Jeff Dunham has made north of $140 million over the last 20 years with a variety of dummies.

I can, however, put a sock over my hand and turn it into a

talking sock that tells jokes. I've earned squat from this prowess, yet it provides a moment of joy for a child, as does another of my skills—honed by hours of disciplined practice—namely, making a nickel or quarter disappear, then producing it from the ear of the child or, in more jocular moments, snorting the coin out my nose.

Yes, I am a man of many non-monetizable skills.

But look, non-monetized skills give life zest. Can you juggle? Wiggle your ears? Impersonate Christopher Walken?

Speaking of which, I loved the impersonators who'd show up on *The Ed Sullivan Show*. Ironically, one of the most popular imitations was of Ed Sullivan himself, because he was easy to do—you just raised your shoulders and made your voice a deeper version of Kermit the Frog and announced outrageous acts. I, of course, did a killer Ed Sullivan—still do, in fact, though the population of people who actually remember Ed Sullivan is dwindling rapidly—and would introduce acts like this: "Tonight on our shooo we have the entire female population of Guadalajara singing a medley of tunes from *Oklahoma!*"

My favorite among the impersonators was Frank Gorshin, who could mold his face into facsimiles of his subjects. He'd show a smiling mouthful of teeth for Burt Lancaster, and gritted teeth for Kirk Douglas, and do a bit where they talked to each other. I stole both of these and amused my Junior High history teacher with them.

Again, for no money. But it may have influenced my grade.

"Life isn't about waiting for the storm to pass. It's about learning to dance in the rain." – Vivian Greene

LIGHTNING BOLTS IN THE HANDS OF ZEUS

Axel Wilhelm Christiansen died at the age of 89. According to his obit he was "a successful plumber" known for his "kind demeanor," and those two things go together quite nicely, for to be an unsuccessful plumber with a kind demeanor is little consolation to the person with a clogged toilet, while being a successful plumber who is unpleasant is a trial even when a hearty flush is restored. Of the two, of course, one would choose the grouchy success over the nice failure, as happens often in life. If you are to get a heart bypass would you want your surgeon to be successful yet dour, or happy yet clumsy?

A man named Paul Wendell Danforth died in Des Moines at the age of 94. He would say, "I'm feeling marvelous" when greeting people well into his 90s.

His obit says he lived a life of "gratitude, faith, family and service to his community." That's a powerful foursome to have in your pocket. To wake up and think about what you're thankful for is balm to the heart. A nourishing faith is comfort for the soul.

And what can take the place of family? Although there are what's called "black sheep" in every family if you go back far enough. On my mother's side there were three sisters—my mom's mom and her two sisters—and a brother. The brother was the black sheep, gambling, drinking and the like, and went off one day and no one knew where. One of my mom's aunts, the youngest one, was close to the brother and missed him, but that's how life goes sometimes, the missing, the hole in the heart...but then, one day out of the blue (blue being the color of surprise for some odd reason, more on that below) the brother showed up at the family home...missing one arm...and the only one there was the oldest sister, the mean one, the one who would have beaten Jane Eyre with a stick if she had shown up in the Brontë novel, and she refused to let him in the house, told him he was not wanted there, and to never darken their doors again. He never did, and when the youngest sister found out what her older sister had done, she never forgave her.

Somehow it doesn't seem like Paul Wendell Danforth would give that kind of reception to a black sheep in his family who showed up years later wanting to make things right. He would have embraced him like the father embraced the prodigal son.

Back to "out of the blue." Why is blue the surprise color? The complete idiom is "like a bolt out of the blue," meaning you're there under a blue sky, the birds are singing, and all seems right with the world, when for no apparent reason a lightning bolt shoots out of the sky and immolates the tree you're sitting under, or the cheese sandwich you're about to eat, or maybe even you if you're holding a golf club, but in any event it's a shock (so to speak).

That's how the Greeks thought about it, the lightning bolts, thrown by Zeus when he was miffed, which was a lot because the Greek gods were just like us, only bigger and more powerful up there on Olympus.

Zeus was a real punk, especially to poor Prometheus, who brought fire to the earth to benefit mankind. Zeus chained him to a rock and had an eagle swoop down, peck out his liver and eat it. Overnight Prometheus grew a new liver, and the whole thing repeats for eternity.

Yes, a barrel of laughs, that Zeus.

Better is "The Beer Barrel Polka," the song popularized in WWII by the legendary Andrews Sisters. That's the one where we roll out the barrel and we'll have a barrel of fun *and* keep the blues on the run!

Over in Cochise County, AZ, a man named Roy Zuckerman died. He was 91 and died of "natural causes," which is a curious phrase implying that nature is out there ready to cause death, but what is so natural about it? Is it just the running down of the machine, the car's transmission giving out so you roll to a stop on the highway of life? The heart stops its gentle thrum, it's had enough, and in having enough you have had enough, too?

Pascal said the heart has its reasons which reason knows nothing of. So I guess when it decides to stop it has its reasons, but we know nothing of it until it actually stops, and by then we're beyond doing anything about it.

So take good care of your heart now, kids, and you could have good run like Mr. Zuckerman, who served in the U.S. Army in Korea, in the Signal Corp, and learned Morse Code, which is a dying dodo of a skill to know anymore, but was handy during the fight against the commies in the North. Later he went to Japan where he met and fell in love with a Japanese woman named Mitsue Kezuka. They were married, which was not an easy thing to do in those days, as the Army discouraged and sometimes prevented it, and if you want to see what that was like there's a movie called *Sayonara* starring Marlon Brando which has a subplot involving Red Buttons and Miyoshi Umeki as a soldier and young Japanese woman who fall in love and have all sorts of trouble, and it ends tragically in the movie, but triumphantly in life, for at the Oscars that year Miss Umeki won the award as Best Supporting Actress.

Thus, always remember the wisdom of that song from *Damn Yankees,* a song Pascal himself might have hummed had he lived long enough to see the show.

> You gotta have heart.
> All you really need is heart.
> When the odds are saying you'll never win
> That's when the grin
> Should start!

"The public will believe anything, so long as it is not founded on truth." – Edith Sitwell

WOULD YOU LIKE YOUR NAUGHTY BOY PIE WITH ICE CREAM OR CHEESE?

Random word: *Pie*.

Who doesn't love a nice slice of pie? There's a pie for every taste, every occasion. There's Apple, Pumpkin, Key Lime, Banana Cream, Coconut Cream. There's Chiffon and Shoofly, Pecan and Sweet Potato. And any kind of berry you choose can be baked in a pie.

Even four-and-twenty blackbirds were once baked in a pie, and so hardy were those birds that when the pie was opened the birds began to sing. Which probably put the king right off his appetite.

But did you know that the first iteration of this rhyme appeared in 1744 with a slightly different lyric, to wit:

Sing a Song of Sixpence,
A bag full of Rye,
Four and twenty Naughty Boys,
Baked in a Pie.

How's that for a little ditty to sing to the kids before bed? "Now be good little boys and girls or you'll end up cooked and stuffed into a pastry, speared with a fork, and eaten. Sweet dreams."

Somewhere along the way a sane person changed *Naughty Boys* to *Blackbirds*, which is also a mystery. Why blackbirds and not flamingos?

We'll probably never know, but we don't need to. The key to the whole thing is *pie*.

I love me some pie, my favorite being apple pie a la mode. This is the quintessential American dessert. You don't hear people going around saying "As Swedish as apple pie" now, do you?

That's because apples were the bumper crop in our growth as a nation. That's why we don't have a myth about Johnny Kumquatseed.

A 1903 editorial in the *New York Times* asserted that eating pie only twice a week was insufficient, "as anyone who knows the secret of our strength as a nation and the foundation of our industrial supremacy must admit. Pie is the American synonym of prosperity, and its varying contents the calendar of changing seasons. Pie is the food of the heroic. No pie-eating people can be permanently vanquished." (Send a note to the Pentagon. *Fewer tanks, more pie.*)

Yet another mystery presents itself. Instead of ice cream, some people actually eat their apple pie a la *cheese*. I have witnessed this first hand, watching the malfeasant mastication with a mix of morbid curiosity and horror.

Yet it, too, has a history. One culinary scholar states:

> The idea appears to have originated in England, where all sorts of fillings were added to pies. At some point, the 17th-century trend of adding dairy-based sauces to pies

morphed into a tradition of topping them with cheese....New England settlers brought the idea behind these Yorkshire pies with them, but instead of Wensleydale, they began using cheddar.

Why cheese? At the time, apple pies were quite bland: prior to the creation of the Red Delicious apple in the late 19th century, few apples tasted sweet. Cheese offered a readily available supplement. After all, in an era before the ubiquity of freezers, the most popular pie topping today—ice cream—was out of the question.

Places in the United States with heavy concentrations of dairy farms therefore became centers of the cheese-on-apple-pie craze. These included New England, Pennsylvania, and especially the Midwest—largely the regions where cheddar cheese apple pie is popular today. (*Source*: Atlasobscura.com)

Apparently, states the above author, Vermont even has a law on the books requiring proprietors of apple pie to make a "good faith effort" to serve it with ice cream, cold milk, or "a slice of cheddar cheese weighing a minimum of 1/2 ounce." This law gives new meaning to the phrase, "Cheese it! The cops!"

Before I die, should I give it a try? It will take some convincing.

I'm a big banana cream pie fan. A famous Valley restaurant near my childhood home was My Brother's Bar-B-Q on Ventura Boulevard. It had a big cow on its sign and served fantastic BBQ beef sammies. But they also had the biggest, fluffiest banana cream pies in the world. Alas, it finally closed after 60 years. At least the owner donated the cow sign to the Valley Relics Museum so I can visit it any time I want.

Via the online game Connections, which I play every day, I learned of two pies with which I was not familiar—chess pie and whoopie pie.

Chess pie came to the American colonies from England. It's apparently like cheesecake, which is where the name may have come from. But since it is mostly a concoction of the deep South, many assert that the name derives from a regional pronunciation: "It's jess pie, y'all." That's probably right, bless their hearts.

Whoopie pie comes from the northeast. It's made up of two round chocolate cake pieces with a creamy white filling, which is why it's sometimes called BFO—Big Fat Oreo. Its origins are controversial. Some say it goes back to a recipe of Martha Washington, which may explain why George had wooden teeth. Pennsylvania claims it was handed down by the Amish, making this state the rightful "home of the whoopie pie."

Maine, however, will have none of that. In 2011 the

Maine Legislature passed a measure that declared the whoopie pie the official state "treat." Glad we have at least some politicians willing to tackle crucial issues head on!

Whoopie is not to be confused with *Whoopee,* which is a word for, ahem, physical congress between a man and a woman. It was the basis for a 1929 song performed by comedian Eddie Cantor, who was often described as "pie-eyed."

The song begins by purporting to celebrate marriage:

Another bride,
Another groom,
Another sunny honeymoon,
Another season,
Another reason
For making whoopee.

But it quickly changes tone:

The chorus sings, "Here comes the bride."
Another victim is by her side.
He's lost his reason cause it's the season
For making whoopee.

Alas, the poor bride:

Another year or maybe less
What's this I hear?
Well, can't you guess?
She feels neglected so he's suspected
Of making whoopee.

It ends in divorce court with the judge announcing a burdensome alimony should the decree be granted:

He says, "Now judge, suppose I fail?"
The judge says, "Bud, right into jail.
You better keep her.
You'll find it's cheaper
Than making whoopee."

   I, on the other hand, have been happily married for 44 years. My wife is my sweetie pie.

"Poets have been mysteriously silent on the subject of cheese." – G. K. Chesterton

CUTTING THE MUSTARD BEFORE THE REAPER DROPS IN

Robert Redford died. Some call him "the last movie star" and there may be something to that (though Clint is still with us). He hearkens back to a time when movie stars were glamorous on the big screen, but since people watch more on TVs and tablets and phones now, it's difficult to create that magic persona we used to identify with Cary Grant and Clark Gable, Bogart and Bacall, Elizabeth Taylor and Richard Burton, Brando and Paul Newman.

In college I had a little black-and-white TV in my dorm room, upon which I once watched *Lawrence of Arabia*. Ha! Meant to be seen in glorious 70mm and in color, David Lean's classic loses a little something on a six-inch screen of mild grays and whites.

The amazing thing about *Lawrence* is that it was shot without computer generated imaging. All those camels charging into Aqaba! One of the most amazing sequences ever filmed, and I wonder if something went wrong and David Lean had to shout, "Cut! Let's take it again!"

The movie made Peter O'Toole a big star, and the guy

could flat out act. He was nominated seven times for an Academy Award and never took home the statuette, a terrible oversight. The same could be said of Richard Burton (also seven nominations) who, along with Elizabeth Taylor, gave actors everywhere an acting clinic in *Who's Afraid of Virginia Woolf*. Liz won for Best Actress, but Burton lost to Paul Scofield in *A Man for All Seasons*. In 1978 Burton was nominated for his powerful performance in *Equus* but lost to Richard Dreyfuss in the light comedy *The Goodbye Girl*. That hardly seems cricket (*cricket* being a British euphemism for "fair"—and to understand why, you must learn the rules of cricket, which no one understands, thus putting you in an endless loop of despair and frustration such as one experiences from, oh, watching the evening news or having a teenager in the home).

O'Toole and Burton possessed magnificent theatrical voices, especially suited to Shakespeare. Patrick Stewart has another such instrument. I found this out personally.

I took a Shakespeare class in college under a legendary professor named Homer Swander. He was chums with the Royal Shakespeare Company. One day our class was surprised by two visitors who came into the lecture hall and greeted Dr. Swander. They were in Southern California preparing for a Los Angeles production of one of the plays (I forget which one). The two actors had recently performed the roles of Brutus and Cassius in *Julius Caesar* in London, which Dr. Swander had seen.

Our prof told us all this, then politely asked the two thespians if they might perform the scene in Act 4 where Brutus and Cassius argue bitterly. The pair expressed surprise at the request, but agreed.

So there we were, this class of Shakespeare enthusiasts, about to watch two magnificent Shakespearean actors—one dressed in blue jeans and a plain white T-shirt, and the other in black pants and a button-up casual—give us a private performance.

I especially noted the blue jeans actor's voice. It was magnificent. He was lean and mostly bald, with a hawk-like face. Many years later I saw that face and heard that voice on television, and knew then it was Patrick Stewart I'd seen in that lecture hall at UCSB. (The other actor was another famous RSC member, John Wood. You may remember him best as the recalcitrant genius hunted down by Matthew Broderick and Ally Sheedy in the movie *War Games*.)

Our "final" for the Shakespeare class was an all-nighter where the students performed scenes from the plays. I got the scene where Hamlet tells Ophelia, "Get thee to a nunnery." (I played Hamlet.)

"To a nunnery go, and quickly, too! Farewell!" (I tried that line once in an argument with my wife, and lost.)

You can now get a college English degree without reading one line of Shakespeare. Talk about not being cricket! How are these future baristas of America expected to understand me when they ask what I'd like and I, staring at the menu, say, "It's Greek to me. My wit's as thick as a Tewkesbury mustard."

Mustard, of course, is a condiment that is spread or squirted upon a bun. So how did we ever get the phrase "cut the mustard" to refer to being "up to snuff" (and where did that latter phrase come from? Interestingly, from an 1810 send-up of *Hamlet*, proving once again that the Bard is foundational for almost everything we say)?

Now, mustard plants used to be cut by hand with a scythe, that tool carried around by The Grim Reaper. If the blade was dull, it wouldn't cut the mustard. You hope that when The Reaper walks by your house his blade is dull.

"Don't fear The Reaper," sang Blue Oyster Cult. That's the song parodied in a famous SNL skit, with Christopher Walken pleading, "I need more cowbell!"

The priority in every life should be to get your inner house in order so you don't fear The Reaper, not like the villain Stalin, whose daughter Svetlana told an interviewer, "My father died a difficult and terrible death. God grants an easy death only to the just. At what seemed the very last moment, he suddenly opened his eyes and cast a glance over everyone in the room. It was a terrible glance, insane or perhaps angry. His left hand was raised, as though he were pointing to something above and bringing down a curse on us all. The gesture was full of menace. The next morning he was dead."

"A man properly must pay the fiddler. In my case it so happened that a whole symphony orchestra had to be subsidized." – John Barrymore

WHAT I LEARNED FROM ROD SERLING

Submitted for your approval, the greatest TV show of all time: *The Twilight Zone*.

It was the brainchild of Rod Serling, who served as executive producer and host of the anthology series. He had a voice like a modulated tension wire, with which he delivered the intro and outro of each episode. He also wrote 92 of the 152 scripts, an amazing output considering the fresh twists and turns that were the hallmarks of the *Zone*. Two other prolific contributors were Charles Beaumont and Richard Matheson, each of whom wrote some of the most memorable offerings. With writers like that it is no wonder the show was high in the ratings from 1959 to 1964.

And it's a gift that keeps on giving, as each new generation gets to discover it via the July 4th "marathons" on the Syfy and Heroes & Icons networks, not to mention streaming. You'll also see many famous actors early in their careers, like Robert Redford, William Shatner ("There's a man on the wing!"), Robert Duvall, Jack Warden, Martin Landau, Leonard Nimoy, Elizabeth Montgomery, Charles Bronson,

Lee Marvin and on and on. Sometimes the actors were in the twilight of their careers, like Ed Wynn and Buster Keaton.

Rod Serling

I was a bit too young to appreciate the original airings, but the show has never been out of reruns. When I did see them, the impact was palpable.

I'll never forget the profound gut punch I felt when I first watched "Time Enough at Last" (written by Serling) which is consistently voted the most memorable episode. That's the one with Burgess Meredith, and I shan't get within miles of revealing the twist. Hunt it down and watch before you read anything about it. (This should be your ironclad rule for any episode of *Zone*!)

Equally stunning was the other episode voted near the top, "Eye of the Beholder" (Serling).

For you youngsters out there who've never seen a *Zone*, let me say I envy you! You've got some incomparable experiences waiting for you. As a public service, I shall give you my personal list of favorite episodes (adding to the two just mentioned):

- "The Howling Man" (Beaumont)
- "Nightmare at 20,000 Feet" (Matheson)
- "The Hitch-Hiker" (Serling)
- "Perchance to Dream" (Beaumont)
- "The Monsters are Due on Maple Street" (Serling, and an episode that absolutely speaks to us today)
- "It's a Good Life" (Serling)
- "To Serve Man" (Serling and Damon Knight)

And my all-time favorite, the second episode of the first season, written by the great Serling, "One for the Angels." I shall give you here Serling's outro which does not contain spoilers, but sums up the heart of the episode:

> Lewis J. Bookman, age sixtyish. Occupation: pitchman. Formerly a fixture of the summer, formerly a rather minor component to a hot July. But, throughout his life, a man beloved by the children, and therefore, a most important man. Couldn't happen, you say? Probably not in most places – but it did happen…in the Twilight Zone.

Ed Wynn in "One for the Angels"

I've long thought a good personality test would be knowing a person's favorite *Zone*. So what does this episode tell me about me? That I'm a lot like Rod Serling.

He had a soft heart and many of his episodes end on a redemptive note. That's me. I love redemption. And justice.

Which reminds me that Serling wrote the script for one of my favorite political thrillers, *Seven Days in May*. What a cast! Burt Lancaster, Kirk Douglas, Fredric March, Ava Gardner, Edmond O'Brien, Martin Balsam. I won't give any spoilers here, but if you like you can hop over to my

Substack and see what I wrote about it (reproducing one of the great movie lines of all time!)

The lesson for a writer is that twists and turns that are tightly woven into the plot are golden threads of reading pleasure. But what makes that gold truly glitter is *heart*.

Rod Serling came to prominence in 1950s television, evincing a heart for the working stiff, especially the "corporation man." Several of his episodes dealt with the pressures on executives and salesmen. "A Stop at Willoughby" is a notable example. Here's the intro:

> This is Gart Williams, age thirty-eight, a man protected by a suit of armor all held together by one bolt. Just a moment ago, someone removed the bolt, and Mr. Williams' protection fell away from him, and left him a naked target. He's been cannonaded this afternoon by all the enemies of his life. His insecurity has shelled him, his sensitivity has straddled him with humiliation, his deep-rooted disquiet about his own worth has zeroed in on him, landed on target, and blown him apart. Mr. Gart Williams, ad agency exec, who in just a moment, will move into the Twilight Zone—in a desperate search for survival.

Serling is one of my heroes. Whatever I write, I always try to do it his way—tap into the lifeblood pumping through my heart.

SCAMMERS, SNAKE OIL SALESMEN, AND O. J. SIMPSON

Random word: *Scam*.

Ah, remember the good old days of Nigerian prince emails you could identify by the fractured English? "All your base are belong to us" and so on?

Well, the age of Artificial Intelligence has cleaned all that up. Now Phan, working in a cubicle in Malaysia, can generate phishing emails in an AI chatbot that sound like they were written by George F. Will.

I got one of these the other day. The email starts off by saying she (a female name) "came across your book" and was "truly struck" by the "raw emotion and depth of storytelling." And that I "deserve" to have my book reach a wider audience. (Well, she's right so far.)

The email goes on to promise higher book rankings on Amazon and a "customized campaign" to increase exposure across "key global markets." Indeed, she has "just worked with an author in a similar genre" who experienced a measurable increase in sales (but doesn't tell us who the author is). She invites me to receive a "complimentary review" of my current Amazon presence and "explore" how the company can help me out. The email signs off with *Warm regards*, followed by the name…but no link to a website (which, of course, does not exist).

What these mills are doing, of course, is using AI to scrape information about writers and their books from the web and generating emails full of praise to prompt a dopamine hit.

We writers are getting such emails daily. Annoying as gnats and reality shows.

Of course, there have always been scammers, con artists, liars and thieves. And that's just in Congress.

In biblical times, the era of the patriarchs, you had that smoothie Jacob (and I do mean that literally. The King James version reports that Jacob was a "smooth man" while his big brother, Esau, was a "hairy man." This led to the ruse used on their dying dad, Isaac by Jacob, at Mom's urging. Jacob went in to see him. Isaac's eyes were failing, and he asked the boy to step forward so he could touch him. He wanted to know if it was Esau, his favorite because Esau loved sports and hunting and Schlitz, while Jacob preferred to make cupcakes with his mother. So Isaac gave his blessing to the fake Esau, Jacob, and the two lines of descent have been at each other ever since).

The women had their little ruses. That Philistine hair stylist, Delilah, played the gullible Samson like a fiddle. But my favorite is Jael, who coaxed the Canaanite general Sisera into her tent, gave him some warm milk, and let him take a nap. She then got a tent peg and hammered it through his skull, the first example of "sticking it to the man."

Of course, the first and worst was the serpent in the Garden, laying his flim-flam on Eve. He's been at it ever since with, sadly, much success.

Deception to make a sale has long been a virus in the bloodstream of commerce. The "snake oil salesman" in the Old West laid out a line of gab about his elixir, sure to cure most ills. It was called snake oil because it was supposedly made by boiling rattlesnakes and skimming off the oil that rose to the surface.

Where in the world did that idea come from? From the

Chinese who arrived as laborers in the 1840s to build the Transcontinental Railroad.

> They would almost certainly have brought with them oil from the Chinese water-snake ... which in traditional Chinese medicine has been used for centuries as an anti-inflammatory agent to treat arthritis, bursitis and other joint pains. These labourers may have offered snake oil to fellow workers as relief for enduring long days of physical effort.
>
> Modern-day research suggests that Chinese water-snake oil may indeed have health benefits because of its high content of omega-3 fatty acids....Omega-3 fatty acids have been shown to reduce inflammation and are alleged to offer many other health benefits.
>
> THE PHARMACEUTICAL JOURNAL, JAN. 23, 2015

So the snake oil salesmen went from town to town hawking their cure-all, which certainly did not contain snake oil. It was more like a combination of mineral oil, beef fat, red pepper, turpentine and a bit of rye whiskey. Tasty! But it didn't get rid of "the rheumatiz."

To sell it, you had to be skilled in the art of charismatic lying.

In my acting days I looked for part-time gigs to pay the bills, and got a job in a "boiler room," a floor of cubicles with phones where the sales force made cold calls to stationary stores claiming to be from a company that was overstocked on Bic pens and the like. We had scripts. The guy in the cubicle next to mine was another struggling actor, and read his lines with Oscar-worthy sincerity.

I made one call and felt so loathsome inside I quit. I became a lawyer, because all lawyers tell the truth.

Ahem.

Jurors hate liars. If they think a witness is lying it's almost always game over for that side.

Remember the O. J. Simpson trial? If you were born before 1980, you certainly do. Many say the turning point was that unforgettable moment when the prosecution called on Simpson to try on the infamous "bloody glove" in open court. "If it doesn't fit, you must acquit," said lead attorney Johnny Cochran in his closing argument.

But your humble scribe thinks the prosecution's case blew up with the cross-examination of Detective Mark Fuhrman by the wily old lion, F. Lee Bailey. Bailey baited Fuhrman into a denial that he had ever used the N word in the last ten years.

But there were tapes. A woman named Kathleen Bell (no relation) wanted to write a novel and she interviewed Fuhrman. Yep, on the tapes he uttered that awful word several times. Worse, Bell asserted that Fuhrman had told her "he would like nothing better than to see all n****s gathered together and burned."

The prosecution never recovered. Juror Carrie Bess said afterward, "Up until they brought the tapes out, I thought O. J. was gone." [The above taken from the book *Outrage: The Five Reasons Why O. J. Simpson Got Away With Murder* by Vince Bugliosi, the man who had prosecuted Charles Manson.]

My thriller series hero, Mike Romeo, has a Latin phrase tattooed on his arm: Vincit Omnia Veritas—Truth conquers all things.

Do we still believe that? We'd better, for it's the only thing that can save us.

And that ain't snake oil.

"If you look for truth, you may find comfort in the end; if you look for comfort you will not get either comfort or truth, only soft soap and wishful thinking to begin, and in the end, despair." – C. S. Lewis

EDISON MEDICINE AND THE HITCHHIKER FROM HELL

Random word: *Medicine.*

Hippocrates (460 BC - 375 BC) is rightly designated "the father of medicine" (aka "the dad of drugs" and "the papa of prescriptions"). He was the first to use observation, rational thought and illegible handwriting to determine what made people sick.

He was famous for defining "the four humors"—puns, one-liners, gags, and knock-knocks. Later, he found four humors in the body, which he admitted were not very funny: yellow bile, black bile, blood and phlegm (ironically, this was also the name of a law firm in Athens).

Hippocrates also came up with the Hippocratic Oath, which he shouted one day after hitting his thumb with a hammer.

We are often told we must "take our medicine." That means admitting to a fault, or revealing an embarrassing or even illegal incident and bearing the consequences. Criminals today are loath to take their medicine, which is why we have police. Indeed, the police have a term for when they use a Taser, the gun that zaps and incapacitates you with electrodes. They call it "Edison medicine."

This refers, of course, to Thomas Alva Edison, the American inventor who brought electric lights into wide use. It was a great advance in civilization, but with the consequence that our land must house an increasingly large "electrical grid." The grid is being tested to the max these days with the rise of EVs. Plug-and-play cars are ubiquitous, racing onto freeways with blinding speed but needing to stop for regular injections of juice.

In the good old days, if your car ran out of gas you opened the trunk, got a gas can and walked to the nearest filling station. But with electric cars, you have to know where the nearest charging dock is, or else drive with a very long extension cord.

Either way, the pull on our electrical grid is like a 380 pound NFL offensive lineman sucking the last bit of milkshake through a paper straw. And that's not the only suck going on. The upsurge in Artificial Intelligence requires bigger data centers, and data centers require...wait for it... electricity. Which is why nuclear energy, especially by way of small modular reactors, is being floated as an efficient solution.

Except in California, where efficient solutions are against the law. That's why we still have a high-speed rail project in the works after 17 years, $15 billion spent, a projected shortfall of $100 billion and no track laid. What's not to love?

I'm old enough to remember streetcars in Hollywood, the kind with a long, spring-loaded pole that contacted an overhead wire. They disappeared in the early 60s with the rise of gas-powered buses, private automobiles, and hippies. The hippies were powered by LSD.

My childhood home was only a few miles from the Spahn Ranch where that adorable gang of misfits known as the Manson Family hung out. You all know what happened. On August 9, 1969, papa Charles ordered four followers—Susan Atkins, Patricia Krenwinkel, Linda Kasabian and Randall "Tex" Watson—to go to the home of actress Sharon Tate and her husband, director Roman Polanski. There they knifed to death the pregnant Tate and four of her friends. Roman was not there at the time.

The next day the crew, along with Manson and another follower, Leslie Van Houten, went to the home of Leno and Rosemary LaBianca, grocery store owners. When police found their bodies the word *war* was carved into Leno's stomach and *Helter Skelter* scrawled on their refrigerator in blood.

"Helter Skelter" was a song by the Beatles that Manson believed held a secret code about a coming race war. It is also the title of the book about the murders and the trial by the chief prosecutor, Vince Bugliosi. It is still the scariest book I've ever read because this wasn't any Stephen King nightmare fiction. It really happened.

The trial was a complete circus. I can still see the zombie eyes of the Manson women, who had carved Xs on their foreheads.

My oldest brother was himself a hippie at the time and favored a motorcycle as his means of transportation. One day he picked up a hitchhiking girl who needed a ride to...the Spahn Ranch. She invited my brother to stay and party with any of the girls. Manson wasn't there. She showed him maps that were plans to escape into the desert after the coming race war. She was recruiting him, using the girls as bait. The scene was too weird and he got out of there.

Six weeks later, after the murders, he recognized a picture of the hitchhiker—Susan Atkins.

Friends, sometimes a Whimsical Wandering takes a turn into doleful territory. But if you want to know what that whole vibe felt like, it was captured perfectly by writer-director Quentin Tarantino in his movie *Once Upon a Time in Hollywood*. There's a scene where Brad Pitt drives a hitchhiking girl to the Spahn Ranch and it is spot on. (Insert "mature audiences only" advisory here.)

Life is made up of moments, some of which have significance we cannot appreciate until later. My big brother might have ended up on the front page of the *L.A. Times* along with Susan Atkins, Tex Watson and the others. But something told him to flee. I believe it was the voice of God, for my brother went on to become a preacher of the Gospel.

Susan Atkins herself claimed to be born again in prison. There are those who think this was a ruse to curry favor with the parole board. If it was, it didn't work. Atkins died in prison in 2009. On the other hand, there is One who knows what was in her heart and whatever mind she had left after years of a brain soaked with drugs. And grace is unlimited.

Let us leave that dark chapter from the past, return to the Whimsy of the present, and end with this. The story is told of a young man on a bicycle riding up to the Mexican border with a backpack. The guard stops him and says, "What's in the backpack?" The guy says, "Sand."

The guard tells him to take off the backpack. He examines it and finds ... nothing but sand. He gives it back and the guy rides across the border.

A week later, same guy rides up. The guard searches the

backpack. Again, nothing but sand, and the fellow rides on. This repeats every two weeks for six months.

The guard quits. One day he's sitting in a San Diego deli and sees the young man. He goes over and says, "Look, you were driving us crazy. We know you were bringing something in. I won't say anything to anybody, but please just tell me what you were smuggling."

"Bicycles."

ON MELTING DOWN

The term "meltdown" was coined in 1956 to describe what could happen if the core of a nuclear reactor overheated. This would cause nuclear fuel to melt and spread radioactive gasses to plants, animals, people, and land. We were in the Cold War then and feared the Russkies could drop a nuclear bomb on us at any moment. In elementary school we practiced "drop drills." We got under our desks with our hands laced over the back of our necks.

But the move toward nuclear power continued apace, with dissenting voices growing more nervous. Then, in 1979, Hollywood got into the act. *The China Syndrome*—starring Jack Lemmon, Jane Fonda and Michael Douglas—depicts an impending meltdown at a nuclear power plant outside Los Angeles. Brave supervisor Lemmon manages to stop it, but not before intrepid reporter Fonda and cameraman Douglas catch the crisis on film. Monied interests want to bury the story, Lemmon gets offed, but a tearful Fonda tells the story on national TV.

Life, as they say, imitates art. The movie got a priceless

jolt of marketing hype when, only a few weeks after its release, there was a partial meltdown at the Three Mile Island nuclear power plant in Pennsylvania. Why, it was almost as if a studio PR hack snuck into the place and turned up the heat himself.

The movie received several Oscar nominations.

Then, in 1986, "the big one" happened. In Ukraine (then part of the Soviet Union) a reactor at the Chernobyl nuclear power plant exploded. Thirty-one workers were immediately fried. Radioactive waste spread across swaths of land. Tens of thousands of people had to be evacuated; thousands developed cancer. The area remains uninhabitable to this day.

But that's not what this essay is about. Indeed, nuclear power is probably the only answer to the voracious electricity needs of proliferating AI data centers and plug-in automobiles.

This about how *meltdown* has come to mean something else—a state of out-of-control idiocy unleashed at full volume and spreading its own excreta of vile waste.

You've no doubt seen or heard about the body cam video from Rhode Island. The Newport police were summoned to a restaurant where a couple of women were asked by the establishment to take a powder. (Interestingly, no one is quite sure why "take a powder" means "to go or get away." Same for "cheese it," as in "Cheese it. The cops!" The only thing we know about the latter is that it has nothing to do with cheese.)

When the gendarmes arrived they met the two women outside and requested that they move along. They refused, things escalated, and they both ended up cuffed and stuffed into police cars.

But not before melting down. Screams issued, F words flew, legs kicked. And one of the recalcitrants turned out to be an Assistant Attorney General of the state of Rhode Island.

This woman kept saying, "I'm an AG! I'm an AG!" and "Buddy, you're gonna regret this. You're gonna regret it." When the officer slapped the bracelets on her she cried, "You're not Mirandizing me!"

Let us pause here for a bit of legal education. Despite what you see on TV, law enforcement is not required to Mirandize arrestees. Indeed, they are trained specifically not to. That's because the Miranda advisement only applies in the context of a custodial interrogation. That means the suspect is in custody *and* is asked *direct questions* about the alleged crime. But at the point of arrest, if they start shouting and yakking, anything they say is admissible in court.

An AG should know that.

So back to melting down. What is it, exactly? It's a psychological explosion (like a core meltdown) wherein the rational part of the brain (assuming there is one to begin with) is obliterated and raw, ragged, inflammatory emotion takes control of body and mind. The meltee becomes a prisoner of their own sound and fury. As Shakespeare's Macbeth puts it:

Life's but a walking shadow, a poor player,
That struts and frets his hour upon the stage,
And then is heard no more. It is a tale
Told by an idiot, full of sound and fury,
Signifying nothing.

In other words, an adult acts like a toddler whose favorite toy has been snatched away and screams, kicks, and holds their breath until they turn blue.

Which is why training for adulthood has to begin by teaching toddlers that such a reaction will always receive a just chastisement. This bit of ancient parental wisdom has somehow become fuzzy and even denied in recent years.

This development was hilariously satirized thirty years ago by the socially observant television program *The Simpsons*. In one episode it's Christmastime and all the kids are enraptured by a new video game called "Bonestorm." The commercial shows two kids in a living room playing a "boring" video game. A buffed-out Santa (think Hulk Hogan in a red suit) blasts through the wall on his sleigh and screams, "You want excitement? Shove this up your stocking!" He pulls out a bazooka and shoots the video game cassette into the console. The game comes up on the screen, showing two combatants relentlessly punching each other as the blood flies.

As Santa prepares to leave he shouts, "So tell your folks, Buy me! Bonestorm! Or go to hell!"

We next see Bart going to his mom in the kitchen. "Buy me Bonestorm or go to hell."

"Bart!" says Marge.

Homer chimes in to teach his son a lesson. "Young man, in this house we use a little word called *please*."

Soon we cut to a scene where a "Rich Suburban Mom" is in a store with her "Spoiled Little Boy (Gavin)." She is dressed like a Malibu Barbie, while the boy has fashionable 90s hair—parted fringe in front with a rat tail in the back.

From the script:

RICH SUBURBAN MOM: Don't you already have this game?

SPOILED LITTLE BOY (GAVIN): No, Mom, you idiot. I have BloodStorm and BoneSquad and BloodStorm II, stupid.

RICH SUBURBAN MOM: I'm sorry. We'll take a BoneStorm.

GAVIN: Get two. I'm not sharing with Caitlin.

The mom buys two games. And Bart, who witnessed the exchange, mutters, "That must be the happiest kid in the world."

Cut to today when meltdowns occur on a daily basis—in parking lots and stores, restaurants and gyms. And even in the halls of power in our fair land.

And social media? Fuggetaboutit. No nourishment there, just scrambled X.

All we can do is take individual responsibility. For

ourselves and for the children in our charge. Refuse to get sucked into the vortex of darkness. That's why I assiduously avoid confrontations on social media. Once you engage like that you get stuck, branded, and the internet is forever. How many celebrities have we seen tarnish their reputations with mindless, obscenity-laden diatribes online? That sort of hatred over time has an effect. You can see how it twists and ages their faces. It's the opposite of Dorian Gray.

That's why I write Whimsical Wanderings. If I can bring a little joy and relief to readers, I'm happy. My wife is like that. She brings kindness wherever she goes. She lifts spirits in grocery store lines and Post Office windows. I've learned from her.

Just yesterday we were driving and came to a corner. A young man on the sidewalk was approaching and we could have sped on by without slowing him down. But I came to a stop and motioned to the young man to cross. As he did he turned to us, smiled, and nodded "Thank you."

"It doesn't take much," Cindy said. She often says that to me when recounting how someone showed her an act of simple kindness or civility.

Yeah, it doesn't take much. But it can make a world of difference to somebody just when they need it.

And if that sounds fluffy and Pollyanna to your ears, let me put it to you this way: Start acting kinder or go to . . . back to bed.

TIME, TIDE, AND TWO DEAD TREES

Random word: *Tide.*

Tide was my mom's preferred laundry soap. She poured it out just like the ladies in the commercials, as in the one where a clumsy moving man spills chocolate sauce all over new curtains, then watches as the calm housewife restores them with Tide.

The saying "Time and tide wait for no man" is an oldie. Chaucer used a form of it in one of his Canterbury Tales. It next shows up in the 16th century in pretty much looking like it does it today.

The word *tide* in those days meant a section of time, making the saying rather redundant. And let me be very clear and exceedingly understood that I am against needless redundancies because they are unnecessarily repetitive.

The saying holds that time marches on, progress happens, and you'd better get with the program or you'll be left behind.

There's a line in the Alistair Sim version of *A Christmas*

Carol (1951) when the young Scrooge is working for Mr. Fezziwig. Old Fezziwig does not want to sell his business to the "vested interests." A representative of this conglomerate, Mr. Jorkin, tells Fezziwig "time and tide wait for no man."

Fezziwig says that sometimes a business exists to preserve and honor a way of life. Jorkin can't fathom that. (Neither, apparently, can certain marketing divisions of certain companies; but that's just an offhand crack.) Jorkin then lures young Scrooge to join him at the shiny new company.

Don't get left behind! This is the baleful cry of Artificial Intelligence. It's here, it's staying, you will be consigned to the dustbin if you don't embrace every bit of it and hold on for dear life!

All while AI is learning, learning, and figuring out how to replace our dear lives with its own.

Geoffrey Hinton is the Nobel Prize-winning physicist who's been called "The Godfather of AI" for his pioneering work on algorithms for training multi-layer neural networks (I almost understand what that means). But he has qualms (*n.*, 1. Uneasy feeling of doubt, worry or fear; 2. A small fruit that grows on qualm trees). In 2023 Hinton, then 75, resigned from his role at Google so he could speak freely about the risks of AI without implicating the company.

He recently gave a speech where he expressed regret at giving his attention solely to the development of AI without regard to the consequences. He now sees a real possibility that AI could "take us over" (starting with mass unemployment) because "it won't need us anymore."

He offered a novel idea for mitigating the danger: instead of trying to force AI systems into submission, researchers should design them with "maternal instincts" so they will "want" to protect and nurture us. "The systems are going to be much smarter than us...The only good outcome is if they care about humanity the way a mother regards her child."

We are all living in the middle of a Ray Bradbury story. I wonder what laundry soap Mother AI will prefer.

The University of Alabama football team is known as the Crimson Tide (a slight change from the original name, Ocean of Blood. They take their football seriously down there in Tuscaloosa).

Which reminds me of the line from the Marx Brothers movie *Animal Crackers* (1930). Groucho plays the explorer

Capt. Geoffrey T. Spaulding. He regales a crowd with some of his exploits in Africa:

"One morning I shot an elephant in my pajamas. How he got in my pajamas, I don't know. Then we tried to remove the tusks...but they were embedded so firmly we couldn't budge them. Of course, in Alabama the Tuscaloosa, but that is entirely ir-elephant to what I was talking about."

Football is not ir-elephant to the Alabama fans, who love to shout, "Roll Tide!" Especially when they are about to face their bitter rival, Auburn.

One such fan was the late Harvey Updyke. So rabid was he that he named his son Bear, after the legendary Alabama coach Paul "Bear" Bryant. Cute, until his fanaticism drove him to murder two trees.

Toomer's Corner is an Auburn campus landmark that is the central gathering place for students and fans after Auburn victories. Two majestic Southern oak trees once stood there. It was a tradition after a victory to toilet paper the trees, a practice dating back to the 1960s. (We don't know why toilet paper was selected for this ritual, though I suspect hippies were involved.)

In 2010, Auburn beat Alabama in the Iron Bowl, 28-27, after a thrilling comeback. The celebration at Toomer's Corner was especially raucous, which pushed Updyke over the edge.

He bought a bag of Spike 80DF, a herbicide that withers trees by being absorbed through the roots, then flowing into the foliage. One night he went to Toomer's Corner and doused the trees with the deadly mix.

The trees began a slow, agonizing death. All attempts to save them failed. And Ol' Harv wanted the world to know why it was done. Calling himself "Al" he phoned a Birmingham radio talk show and said he'd poisoned the trees because Auburn cheated.

He ended the call by declaring, "Roll damn Tide!"

He was eventually nabbed and pled guilty to "felony criminal damage of an agricultural facility." He served 70 days in the clink and was ordered to pay $800,000 in restitution. They were only able to squeeze $6,900 out of him before his death in 2020.

New oak trees were planted at Toomer's Corner in 2015.

In Shakespeare's *Julius Caesar*, Brutus declares:

> There is a tide in the affairs of men
> Which, taken at the flood, leads on to fortune;
> Omitted, all the voyage of their life
> Is bound in shallows and in miseries.

He's talking to Cassius, post their assassination of Caesar. He means the tide rolls on, no matter what we do, and if we don't catch it we'll be left on shore, missing fortune and gaining only misery.

The dope. In Dante's *Inferno*, do you know who is consigned to the ninth circle of hell? Only three: Brutus, Cassius and Judas Iscariot. They are guilty of treason to their benefactors, the worst of all sins according to the poet. Lucifer, encased in ice, chews them for eternity.

So maybe we should think very carefully about the tides and seek divine wisdom on when to resist them.

I just thought I'd float that idea.

Which brings us to the Whimsical joke that ends our session.

Who was the greatest financial genius in the Bible? Some say it was Pharaoh's daughter. She went to the Bank of the Nile and withdrew a little "prophet." But I say it was Noah, who floated his stock while the rest of the world was in liquidation.

"In times of disorder and stress, the fanatics play a prominent role; in times of peace, the critic. Both are shot after the revolution." – Edmund Wilson

YOU CAN SCARF DOGS BUT YOU CAN'T FAKE COOL

Esther Duran died at the age of 86, in San Antonio. Her obit describes her as "a God-fearing woman who lived her life as a testament to her unwavering love for Jesus." Her "quiet strength and kind spirit left a lasting impact on all who knew her." To live and love and leave an impact, there is no finer legacy than that. Little things can be universes to those we touch, elbow to elbow, even in our own little plot of land on this green earth, people we may not see but once...rather than "elbowing people out of the way" which is a way to live that leaves impact of another kind, a bad kind, like the woman who screamed at a father and son who nabbed a baseball in a game, a ball she believed she had a right to...a *baseball*...a small sphere of cushioned cork and rubber, wrapped in layers of wool and yarn, enclosed by cowhide leather stitched with waxed red thread, something you can get at Walmart for a few bucks.

We don't know how to pick our fights anymore, we fight over toys on a store shelf, we fight over parking spaces... Steven Wright, an existential philosopher inside the body of a comedian, once said, "When I get real bored, I like to drive downtown and get a great parking spot, then sit in my car and count how many people ask if I'm leaving."

I was at an outdoor event recently and seats in the shade were at a premium, and I was sitting next to an old friend, very comfortably, chatting about this and that, when an older woman happened by, searching, and both of us stood up at the same time. Men used to do that on streetcars and buses and subways. I miss those days.

In my acting years in New York, I rode the subway all the time. This was back when you could ride and largely avoid getting killed. The opening song to the movie musical *On the Town* proclaims, "New York, New York! A wonderful town. The Bronx is up and the Battery's down. The people ride in a hole in the ground. New York, New York...it's a wonderful town!"

People don't sing that anymore. New York was much more wonderful when every block in midtown had a Chock-full-o'-Nuts coffee shop next door to a Nathan's Famous Hot Dogs stand. I could start my morning with a "regular" coffee (meaning with cream) and a powdered donut, and get a Nathan's for lunch, with mustard and 'kraut. And I survived, though I cannot explain why contestants in the annual Nathan's Hot Dog Eating Contest don't drop dead. See how many Nathan's dogs—buns included—you can force down your gullet in 10 minutes?

At least it's live theater. I used to love live theater in New York when some good and original plays were still on Broadway and especially Off-Broadway. I saw some great performances—front row for the original *Chicago* with the legendary Gwen Verdon, Chita Rivera and Jerry Orbach. *Evita* with Patti LuPone and Mandy Patinkin. *A Moon for the Misbegotten* with Jason Robards and Colleen Dewhurst, after which I snuck backstage to the dressing rooms and said hello to Robards because he grew up in the house across the street from my dad, and of course he remembered him and welcomed me, and we had a talk about acting.

Robards' career as a respected actor took off in 1956 with an Off-Broadway production of *The Iceman Cometh,* surely the most difficult American play to put on (over four hours, uncut), with the most challenging role, the salesman Hickey and his fifteen-minute, soul-wrenching monologue in the last act. If I could go back in time, that would be the performance I'd want to see most, followed by Laurette Taylor in *The Glass Menagerie,* and Brando and Jessica Tandy in *A Streetcar Named Desire.*

Then I discovered that a live TV performance of *Iceman* was done in 1960, directed by no less than Sidney Lumet. I got the DVD! So I did get to see the performance of a lifetime.

The most impressive live performance I ever saw was Glenda Jackson in *Hedda Gabler,* in Los Angeles. I was in college and some of my fellow film students and I went to see it. Stunning. We slipped backstage to see if we could say hello to Miss Jackson. She welcomed us into the dressing room and was very gracious. As we spoke, a striking woman came in to say hello to the star. A few years later I would see that face again and learn that her name was Anjelica Huston.

I slipped out of the dressing room and there was Anjelica's boyfriend Jack Nicholson, alone, leaning against the wall. I knew he was finishing up *One Flew Over the Cuckoo's Nest* (one of my favorite novels) so I asked him how it was going. He gave me that wry Nicholson smile and said something funny, with a little salty language tossed in (I shan't repeat it) and you know what? He sounded just like Jack Nicholson!

And isn't that how everyone should sound? Like himself

or herself, certainly not some pale imitation of some other self. One time I tried to sound like someone else, like a cool kid, like Nicholson cool—which I wasn't in high school and girls were a mystery—and there was one girl I liked and tried to impress, but she was not impressed with me.

So one day at the lockers I talked to her and she clung to her indifference, so I gave her an exit line I thought would be cool. "Dig you later," I said. The moment it came out of my mouth I felt like I was in clown makeup in the middle of a circus tent. *Dig you later?* That line might have had some heft in 1955, but not 1971.

Unsurprisingly, I never did get a date with that girl. It was not until years later, out of college and in New York, that I finally figured out you need to be yourself, lean into you, get rid of the deadwood, and sandpaper the rough edges—or you can't be authentic to anyone. "Be who you is," wrote Brennan Manning in *Ruthless Trust*. "'Cause if you ain't who you is, you is who you ain't."

Although, for amusement, I can do a killer Nicholson impression.

∼

"Be yourself; everyone else is already taken." – Oscar Wilde

A DUKE, PANSY O'HARA, AND GARBO'S FEET

It occurred to me the other day that I don't know anyone named Horace.

Indeed, I can't recall even meeting anyone named Horace. I read some Horace, the Roman poet, in college. His real name was Quintus Horatius Flaccus, a bit too much to fit on a marquee, so Horace it became.

He is credited with popularizing the Latin phrase *Carpe diem*—Seize the day—good advice for the living of life, the *doing* of life, rather than sitting around like Jabba the Hutt eating Klatooine paddy frogs and belching.

I sometimes get asked for advice from a young writer. Usually I sign off with my own Latin phrase, *Carpe typem*—Seize the keyboard. You cannot learn to write without writing a lot.

Other than Mr. Flaccus, the only other Horaces that come to mind are Horace Greeley, the American newspaper editor; and Horace Walpole, the English politician and writer who also happened to be the 4th Earl of Orford (not a typo). I don't have any idea how they work the Duke and Earl systems over there. I only know the R&B song that was a hit in the 60s and is often played on oldies stations. It begins, "Duke Duke Duke Duke of Earl Duke Duke Duke of Earl Duke Duke Duke of Earl Duke Duke Duke of Earl Duke Duke Duke of Earl." Not exactly Cole Porter, but it gets into your head and keeps repeating "Duke Duke Duke" ...over and over... "Duke of Earl Duke Duke...."

Another song that does the same is "Karma, karma, karma, karma, karma chameleon." Ack!

The only cure I've found for getting rid of these brain peckings is by calling to mind the theme from *Hawaii Five-O*. Knocks any tune right out of your noggin.

It also occurs to me that I've never met any woman named Hortense. Indeed, in my Word program Hortense gets a red underline indicating a spelling error. But it's a legit name derived from the Latin *hortus*, meaning "garden" and thus connotes beauty and growth. It was popular in France for awhile in the 1700s, and in the late 19th century in America. But it's pretty much fallen off the charts since then. The sound is rather hard on contemporary ears. (When I think of contemporary ears I think of King Charles III, which reminds me I've never met a king, either.)

Had I been born a girl my parents were going to name me Bonnie Blue Bell. I am glad I turned out to be a boy. The name comes from Margaret Mitchell's novel *Gone With the Wind* and is the name of Scarlett and Rhett's daughter. Because my dad was an extra in the movie—he's one of the hundreds of wounded soldiers in that big train depot scene—my folks thought that name would have a nice "ring" to it (you'll pardon the pun). However, there is apparently a woman out there named Bonnie Blue who is some sort of superstar in the porn film industry. That Y chromosome saved me from some embarrassing misidentifications.

Speaking of *GWTW*, Margaret Mitchell first called her character Pansy O'Hara. Just before publication a wise editor pleaded with Miss Mitchell to consider a name change. So it became Scarlett by a whisker.

Hildegard is another name you don't hear often, as it belongs primarily to German girls. There was a German actress named Hildegard Knef who had brief success in America in the 1950s, and even scored some of the most precious real estate in Hollywood, namely a square of cement in front of Grauman's Chinese Theater. Many famous movie stars have their hand and footprints there, but why Hildegard Knef back in 1951? Because 20th Century Fox was about to release *Decision Before Dawn*, a movie set in Germany during the final year of WWII. It was Knef's American debut and the comely blonde had a showy supporting role as a German widow who turned to prostitution. The PR department jumped on the chance to turn Knef into another foreign beauty along the lines of Ingrid Bergman.

That didn't happen, but Knef did score a major win on Broadway in *Silk Stockings*, a musical adaptation of the 1939 Greta Garbo comedy *Ninotchka*. That movie was about an ice-cold Soviet envoy (Garbo) whose heart is eventually melted by a charming American (Melvyn Douglas). Garbo is great playing the unsmiling Commie, which fit her onscreen *and* offscreen persona as a dour tragedian who just wanted to be left alone. She retired in 1941, refused all film offers ever after, and lived a long, private life on New York's Upper East Side, given to wearing wide-brimmed hats and shades when going out for a stroll.

She never liked the movie business. Her obsessive introversion drew jokes from others in the industry, including snickering gossip that she had big feet. The hilarious Looney Tunes cartoon "Hollywood Steps Out" (1941) features several caricatures of many stars, including Garbo as a cigarette girl, and Harpo Marx giving her a "hotfoot" by sticking matches in her very large shoes. When the flames reach her foot Garbo's expression doesn't change one bit. She merely utters, "Ouch."

Once, after the Marx Brothers came to Hollywood in the 30s, Groucho got on an elevator in the Thalberg Building at MGM. On the second floor the door opened and a woman wearing a huge hat *backed* into the elevator.

Groucho couldn't resist. He took hold of the back of the hat and folded it up and over the woman's head.

She turned around and shot him a withering look. It was Garbo. And Groucho said, "I'm terribly sorry, I thought you were a fellow I knew from Kansas City."

Years later Groucho told that story to Dick Cavett, and added, "I met her subsequently about ten years later, at a party, and we discussed this, and she was very nice about it. She had big feet, but she was a nice woman."

In the 1920s Groucho Marx lived in a house in Great Neck, Long Island. He inquired about membership at a posh swimming club but was told they had a policy against admitting Jews. He replied, "Well then, how about my son? He's only half Jewish. Can he go in the water up to his waist?"

ME, BOONE'S FARM APPLE WINE, AND MY BEST FRIEND RANDY

The outskirts of Flagstaff, Arizona. I was with my high school church group, taking a week in the summer to do volunteer work on the Hopi reservation. Our bus had stopped for the night and we brought our sleeping bags and duffels into the fellowship hall of a local church. We were told by our adult leaders to relax, read, play games, listen to the radio—but by all means stay inside the hall. Which of course my friend Randy Winter and I interpreted as meaning, "Feel free to wander into town and find some trouble to get into."

Ever ready to follow instructions as we understood them, Randy and I slipped out the side doors and started a nocturnal tour of the bustling Flagstaff metropolis, which seemed to have, as they used to say, rolled up the sidewalks.

So we walked and talked and came to a railroad crossing, and then into the soft red-and-yellow neon of a liquor store sign. To a couple of seventeen-year-olds on a nighttime prowl, such illumination was catnip. Randy suggested we baptize our adventure with a bottle.

I agreed, as Randy was my brother from another mother with whom I laughed much and talked deeply. We would discuss with equal fervor the mystery of girls and the character of God (whose reputation, by the way, we were failing to uphold as we schemed how to lay our hands on some demon intoxicant).

Our first order of business was what manner of spirits to acquire. As an athlete who was not a member of the party circuit, I was not an imbiber of any sort. I did not like the taste of beer. I'd snuck a nip of gin once in my parents' liquor cabinet and wondered why on earth anyone would want to drink gasoline.

So Randy suggested we try some wine. He'd heard that Boone's Farm Apple Wine went down nicely, and the decision was made.

The next step was to lurk in the shadows of the parking lot until a car drove up, then casually approach the driver with a request that he be our procurer. This was nervous time, for who knew what kind of person we would engage? What if it was an off-duty cop? Or some old Veteran of Foreign Wars who'd want to lecture us on the evils of drink?

A chance we would have to take.

Presently, a car turned into the lot. Out stepped a man of about thirty, with long hair. Long hair! A good sign. A hippie perhaps, or at least a musician. In either case, cool. We emerged from our hiding spot and said, "Excuse me ..."

The man stopped and read our faces in the soft, primrose light. "You want me to get you a bottle, don't you?"

We nodded. My face felt flush, as if the entire world were witnessing my iniquity.

The man laughed. "I used to do the same thing. What do you want?"

We gave the man a couple of fins, our pooled resources, and Randy said, "Boone's Farm Apple Wine."

It seemed to me the man hesitated, as if to give us one last chance to reconsider our fate. And then he went through the door.

Randy and I high-fived our success. And soon thereafter we had in our hands a brown paper bag and some change, passed to us with a "Good luck" sentiment from our partner in crime.

We left the scene of our misdemeanor, went back near the railroad tracks, and sat cross-legged on the ground.

Randy unscrewed the top. We were too unsophisticated to smell the cap.

Then he drank and passed the bottle to me. I took a tentative sip. Ah, I thought, conversational without being verbose, with a sprightly fruitiness and subdued notes of summer. (Actually, what I really thought was, *This isn't so bad.*)

And so 'neath the Arizona stars Randy Winter and I shared a bottle of what was generously classified as wine, and discovered something interesting about the human body, namely, that there is a lag time between the ingestion of alcoholic content and its effect on one's physiology.

Which meant, at one point, it suddenly felt as if a switch was flipped in my brain. A disco ball lit up and went round and round, and I heard myself say something like, "Rammy, my headth pinning" before I teetered backward and ended up on the gravel, looking up at the stars as they raced around the heavens like sparkling emergency room nurses shouting, "Stat! Stat!"

Which is the last thing I remember about that night. In the morning I was in my sleeping bag on the church floor. At least I think it was my sleeping bag. My stomach felt like a balloon of toxic gasses. Two miniature railroad workers were on either side of my head, driving spikes into my temples with their sledgehammers.

The adult leaders were none too pleased with Randy and me. We knew we'd messed up, crossed the line, failed to represent our church. We were threatened with expulsion, which would mean a long and humiliating drive for our parents to come pick us up. We threw ourselves upon the mercy of the court and were granted a temporary stay. I began then to truly appreciate the power of forgiveness. Plus, I was ready to swear off booze for good.

Honest, hard work kept Randy and me on the straight and narrow that week. There's a victory in there somewhere.

I was thinking about Randy the other day, as I often do. He died at the age of nineteen. Leukemia. When I think about him, and all the good times we had, this particular memory is the one that surfaces first.

Why is that? Maybe because it typified our friendship. We took risks together, got in trouble on occasion, but mostly laughed. A couple of times there were tears. There's something deeply meaningful to me in all this, and if I explore it I sense it will tell me something about what I write and why.

Early in his career Ray Bradbury started making lists of nouns based on childhood memories. Things like The Lake, The Night, The Crickets, The Ravine.

"These lists were the provocations," he writes in *Zen in the Art of Writing*, "that caused my better stuff to surface. I was feeling my way toward something honest, hidden under the trapdoor on the top of my skull."

When I open up my own trapdoor I find untapped material I can use as the basis for a piece of fiction, or for character emotion and scenes. Nothing is wasted. At the very least I learn something about myself.

I don't believe I've had a taste of Boone's Farm wine since that night. Nothing against it, you understand (well, almost nothing), but I prefer a nice California cab.

In fact, I think I'll have a pour tonight and raise the glass to my best friend, Randy Winter.

MORE BUNS!

Thanks for reading *Cinnamon Buns and Milk Bone Underwear*. For more of the same, you can subscribe to my Substack, Whimsical Wanderings. It's free. A paid subscription will bring you all the content, including the reader-favorite *JSB's Whiz Bang*. Enjoy!

To subscribe, go to:

>jamesscottbell.substack.com/about

ABOUT JAMES SCOTT BELL

James Scott Bell is the multi-bestselling author of thrillers and books on the writing craft, and winner of both the

International Thriller Writers Award and the Christy Award (Suspense). He attended the University of California, Santa Barbara, where he studied writing with Raymond Carver, and graduated with honors from USC Law School. He lives and writes in Los Angeles. His website is JamesScottBell.com.

His thrillers are:

The Mike Romeo Thriller Series
Winner of the International Thriller Writers Award

Visit your Amazon store and search for: **Mike Romeo Series**

"Mike Romeo is a terrific hero. He's smart, tough as nails, and fun to hang out with. James Scott Bell is at the top of his game here. There'll be no sleeping till after the story is over."
— **John Gilstrap**, New York Times bestselling author of the Jonathan Grave thriller series

The Ty Buchanan Legal Thriller Series

#1 Try Dying
#2 Try Darkness
#3 Try Fear

"Part Michael Connelly and part Raymond Chandler, Bell has an excellent ear for dialogue and makes contemporary L.A. come alive. Deftly plotted, flawlessly executed, and compulsively readable. Bell takes his place as one of the top authors in the crowded suspense genre." - **Sheldon Siegel**, *New York Times* bestselling author

The Complete JSB Short Fiction Collection

Down These Streets

The Trials of Kit Shannon Historical Legal Thrillers

Book 1 - City of Angels
Book 2 - Angels Flight
Book 3 - Angel of Mercy
Book 4 - A Greater Glory
Book 5 - A Higher Justice
Book 6 - A Certain Truth

"With her shoulders squared and faith set high, Kit Shannon arrives in 1903 Los Angeles feeling a special calling to practice law ... Packed full of genuine, deep and real characters ... The tension and suspense are in overdrive ... A series that is timeless!" — **In the Library Review**

Stand Alone Thrillers

Can't Stop Me
Your Son Is Alive
Long Lost
No More Lies
Blind Justice
Don't Leave Me
Final Witness

ABOUT JAMES SCOTT BELL

Framed
Last Call

Mallory Caine, Zombie-At-Law Series

You read that right. A new genre. Part John Grisham, part Raymond Chandler—it's just that the lawyer is dead. Mallory Caine, Zombie at Law, defends the creatures no other lawyer will touch...and longs to reclaim her real life.

Pay Me In Flesh
The Year of Eating Dangerously
I Ate The Sheriff